D1624432

Praise for

THE LIFE YOU LONG FOR

"Is your soul tired and worn out? Do you need a new way to live? Christy Nockels is a gentle, strong voice shepherding us into a fuller life with Jesus at the very center. This book will restore your weary soul."

—JENNIE ALLEN, *New York Times* bestselling author of *Get Out of Your Head* and founder and visionary of IF:Gathering

"I have waited and waited for Christy Nockels to write a book. It was worth the wait! There's something about Christy. Always has been. She writes as she sings, bringing a moment's grace, a moment's peace, and a moment's beauty into a world of chaos. Read and rest your weary heart and find gladness in your God again."

—BETH MOORE, speaker, Bible teacher, and bestselling author

"Christy Nockels's life resonates with the melody of authenticity and holiness. This book is Christy's story—the tale of a woman growing in grace and showing us how to do the same. Each chapter shimmers with insights that underscore the spiritual disciplines that are increasingly overlooked and undervalued: abiding in Christ, accepting His love, resting in His providential care, and choosing a lifestyle of contentment. In other words, this book is pure grace. It will draw you to Jesus and remind you about the beautiful song that the Father is writing with your life too."

—PRISCILLA SHIRER, Bible teacher and author

"*The Life You Long For* is the literary equivalent of relaxing in cool crystal-clear water on a really hot and humid day. God has gifted Christy Nockels with such a keenly observant heart and a poetic psalmist kind of voice, which makes her a safe and compelling tour guide into the transformative topography of divine grace. This must-read book is a lovely invitation to lean more fully into the unconditional love of Jesus Christ and to lean with more authentic compassion into the lives of other image bearers."

—LISA HARPER, author and speaker

"Christy Nockels has spurred us on for years through her music and now does so through her own story, and I believe it's right on time. For all of us who know the tension between what's expected of us and what we really long for, Christy gently leads us into true freedom."

—RUTH CHOU SIMONS, mom to six boys, founder of gracelaced.com, and bestselling author of *Beholding and Becoming*

"As I was reading *The Life You Long For,* I felt like I was having coffee with a sweet friend who was constantly reminding me and my heart to rest—not just any sort of rest, but resting in God's love for me and His plans for me. Christy weaves storytelling and truth together in a way that causes you to ponder the overwhelming song of love that the Father sings over each of us."

—JAMIE IVEY, bestselling author and host of *The Happy Hour with Jamie Ivey* podcast

"Christy Nockels is a deep, deep well, and I so appreciate the honesty and vulnerability in her book, *The Life You Long For.* I know it will help you discover the intimacy with God that we all crave and were made for. Thank you, Christy, for pouring your heart and soul into each word and reminding us of what this life is all about."

—CHRIS TOMLIN, singer and songwriter

"In the hustle and grind of life, we can mistakenly believe that our good works and effort curry favor with God. But Christy Nockels's words teach us ever so gently that our striving is exhausting us! *The Life You Long For* is a song for us to learn and sing in our own harmony so our souls can be set free."

—BIANCA JUAREZ OLTHOFF,
speaker, teacher, and bestselling author
of *How to Have Your Life Not Suck*

"Christy Nockels shares from personal experience that tiring ourselves for God is not the same as enjoying being with Him. Through her vulnerable storytelling, Christ-focused truth-telling, and thoughtful biblical perspective, we're told the greatest news on earth: the longing inside us is fulfilled only and wholly in Jesus."

—KELLY MINTER, Bible teacher and
author of *Finding God Faithful*

"Before I met Christy Nockels, I was shaped by her songs and ministry. Once I got to know her personally, I was more deeply affected by her life and friendship, especially her intimate relationship with the Lord. *The Life You Long For* is a compilation of all our coffee dates, late-night chats, long-distance phone calls, and heartfelt emails. If you've ever wanted to sit across from her and glean wisdom from her years of faithful adoration of and intimacy with Jesus, read this book."

—LAUREN CHANDLER,
author, worship leader, and songwriter

"Reading *The Life You Long For* feels like you are sitting with Christy, hearing her kind voice and wise words, laughing along with her as she tells the best stories and the most heartfelt truths."

—ANNIE F. DOWNS,
bestselling author of *100 Days to Brave*

"As a friend, I've watched Christy Nockels live this message in real time, pouring truth into these pages. May her words breathe grace and inspire rest in your soul as you seek the journey God destines for each of us. This book will help you recover your life!"

—REBEKAH LYONS,
bestselling author of *Rhythms of Renewal*

THE
LIFE
YOU
LONG
FOR

CHRISTY NOCKELS

THE
LIFE
YOU
LONG
FOR

LEARNING *to* LIVE
from A HEART *of* REST

MULTNOMAH

All Scripture quotations and paraphrases, unless otherwise indicated, are taken from the ESV® Bible (The Holy Bible, English Standard Version®), copyright © 2001 by Crossway, a publishing ministry of Good News Publishers. Used by permission. All rights reserved. Scripture quotations marked (BSB) are taken from the Holy Bible, Berean Study Bible, BSB. Copyright © 2016, 2018 by Bible Hub. Used by permission. All rights reserved worldwide. Scripture quotations marked (KJV) are taken from the King James Version. Scripture quotations marked (MSG) are taken from The Message. Copyright © 1993, 2002, 2018 by Eugene H. Peterson. Used by permission of NavPress. All rights reserved. Represented by Tyndale House Publishers, a division of Tyndale House Ministries. Scripture quotations marked (NIV) are taken from the Holy Bible, New International Version®, NIV®. Copyright © 1973, 1978, 1984, 2011 by Biblica, Inc.™ Used by permission of Zondervan. All rights reserved worldwide. (www.zondervan.com). The "NIV" and "New International Version" are trademarks registered in the United States Patent and Trademark Office by Biblica, Inc.™ Scripture quotations marked (NLT) are taken from the Holy Bible, New Living Translation, copyright © 1996, 2004, 2015 by Tyndale House Foundation. Used by permission of Tyndale House Publishers, a division of Tyndale House Ministries, Carol Stream, Illinois 60188. All rights reserved.

Italics in Scripture quotations reflect the author's added emphasis.

Copyright © 2021 by Christy Nockels

All rights reserved.

Published in the United States by Multnomah, an imprint of Random House, a division of Penguin Random House LLC.

MULTNOMAH® and its mountain colophon are registered trademarks of Penguin Random House LLC.

Published in association with Yates & Yates, www.yates2.com.

Library of Congress Cataloging-in-Publication Data
Names: Nockels, Christy, author.
Title: The life you long for : learning to live from a heart of rest / Christy Nockels.
Description: First edition. | Colorado Springs, Colorado : Multnomah, 2021.
Identifiers: LCCN 2020011868 | ISBN 9780593192542 (hardcover) |
ISBN 9780593192559 (ebook)
Subjects: LCSH: Christian women—Religious life. | Trust in God—Christianity. |
Rest—Religious aspects—Christianity.
Classification: LCC BV4527 .N63 2021 | DDC 248.8/43—dc23
LC record available at https://lccn.loc.gov/2020011868

Printed in the United States of America on acid-free paper

waterbrookmultnomah.com

First Edition

Interior book design by Jo Anne Metsch

2 4 6 8 9 7 5 3 1

SPECIAL SALES Most Multnomah books are available at special quantity discounts when purchased in bulk by corporations, organizations, and special-interest groups. Custom imprinting or excerpting can also be done to fit special needs. For information, please email specialmarketscms@penguinrandomhouse.com.

. . .

For the Fellowship of the Farm Table:
My Beloved, Nathan, and our treasured children,
Noah, Elliana, and Annie Rose.
Resting with you will always be my favorite!

. . .

And for anyone who's tuckered out from trying and striving,
those who feel like you're worth more when you do more
and build more, and for anyone feeling small because
you had to lay down what you were building.
I get you.
May you find true rest and the Life
that you are longing for.

CONTENTS

THE
LIFE
YOU
LONG
FOR

1

HIS BANNER OVER ME IS LOVE

IMAGINE IF YOU AND I WERE TO SIT DOWN TOGETHER to get acquainted, and before we begin, someone gives us specific parameters for our conversation, guidelines to help us skip the small talk and go straight to the meaningful and memorable stuff. You and I are challenged to introduce ourselves without alluding to anything we do or have done in terms of a vocation or trade. We are told to focus only on our interior lives and matters of the heart.

To be honest with you from the get-go, there was a time in my life when such a challenge would have left me a bumbling mess! While I would have been elated to nix the small talk, I would've felt stripped bare in having to bypass my exterior world and abandon the crutch of my career, which I have a tendency to lean on when describing who I am. Even now, it might take a few stops and starts for me to find the right words to reveal the heart of who I am.

How about you? How would you introduce yourself to me? I wonder what pieces of your story you might reveal, insights that describe the making of *you*. Would you be hard pressed for words, maybe even feel small and unseen, if you had to leave out what you do, or would you be relieved in some ways?

What if, after what I'm sure would be a refreshing and revealing introduction, our mediator proposed another prodding challenge? What if we were asked to describe to each other the life we truly long for? However, as we describe our wants and dreams, we cannot include any milestones, accolades, or any level of success we'd hope to achieve. How would you describe the life you long for?

Would you say that your soul seems to ache with something you can't quite put your finger on? Maybe you've achieved some milestones in your exterior world but you're left with a surprising, insatiable longing for more. Perhaps you've had to lay down your career for a season and that has caused an unrest in your soul.

I think we'd both agree that life has become more complicated than we ever imagined, as everywhere we look, we are inundated with conflicting messages. Some say we should rest, some say we should run wholeheartedly after our dreams and never look back, and some urge us to find the balance in between. We feel pulled in more directions than we even knew existed, having given the world twenty-four-hour instant access to our psyches and our souls.

Have you become weary amid all these competing pressures? Maybe you started out with a pure devotion to pursue the dreams you believe God placed in your heart but lately it's begun to look and feel tainted. How often has our devotion turned into busyness and our commitment turned into a craving for recognition? Everywhere we click and scroll, it seems like everyone's out there doing something big. We feel compelled to take on the pressure to keep building big things too. Then there's our longing for connection with the people in our lives. Yet family can feel like juggling endless practical responsibilities while stewarding sacred relationships. Our longing for community often becomes a struggle against lives stuffed too full to get our calendars lined up. Or maybe we've been burned in some of our dearest relationships. Wounds, both given and received, seem an inevitable result of braving the messy middle of pursuing a life of togetherness.

I've experienced all the above—the chronically over-scheduled life, an imbalance between family and work, the pressure to build big things, and even the complications of trying to achieve authentic community. I lacked the ability to be present for anything in my life as I felt compelled to plow through what I know now were precious seasons, just to get to the next seemingly urgent thing. As a new mom, while I was head over heels in love with my family, I mostly felt in over my head about how to truly care for them when I considered how much I also cared about the things that I felt God had placed in my heart to share with the world.

Inevitably, I reached what felt like the end of my own ability and capacity, and I became thoroughly tired. *Bone tired.*

The kind of tired that robs you and me of the very things we long for in this life—peace, joy, contentment, belonging, and *rest*.

If you and I did get to sit down to explore these questions together, I bet we'd find that we have more in common than we'd imagined. I also bet we'd bump into a bit of mystery as we got to the bottom of the funnel of who we really are. We'd have to acknowledge a certain sanctity to our lives that we sense but can't quite put words around, as well as a longing we're still trying to define. I believe that at some point in our conversation, our Belovedness would inevitably peek through our peripheral shells and the stuff of real life would start spilling out.

Beloved. (I'm going to call you this quite often, so you might want to go ahead and try it on and see how it feels.) This is the one big something that I know is true of you: you are God loved, which is essentially what the name Beloved means. I find it beautiful that God both *made* us in His image and *named* us in His image. First John 4:8 says, "God is love," and then all throughout Scripture you and I are called Beloved—or as the Greek says, "loved by God."[1] It's as if we're the response to who He is, and right from the start, He is the fulfillment of our greatest need: *to be loved.*

You've likely seen this name Beloved in Scripture. You might even have worn it on a T-shirt or a necklace. But maybe you've become a bit numb to its true hold on you. What if I told you that living from your Belovedness changes everything? That it could unfold the *true you* as well as give you an unimagined capacity to be about the things of God and the life you've longed for. If I showed you how the true you could emerge from a place of contentment and rest, would you be willing to crawl into this kind of chrysalis and yield to the process?

There is such a place, and I'm grateful beyond words that God called me to it, to be able to experience the catapulting capacity of His rest. It was here that I discovered what He truly requires of me and also what He doesn't. It was here that I was surprised to find what is most valuable to Him as well as some things that I didn't know were priceless to me. I was also blown away to discover that in finding true rest in God, I'd watch Him unfold the life I was longing for in a way that I could never have dreamed or planned.

MEETING GOD IN THE BROKENNESS

At the end of 2017, I found myself wanting to hold on to every last bit of cozy that celebrating Christmas brings but also ready to kick to the curb all the clutter that I could see piling up in my house. We had gotten quite merry with decking the halls that year, especially because we were celebrating our tour for my first Christmas album. Yet, in the after-Christmas glow, I began to crave the clean slate of remembering Jesus in the form of a fresh year and a new beginning. So I made plans. Like, hit-the-ground-running kind of plans for the new year:

Word for the year? Check!

Game plan to purge my house of clutter? Check!

Themes laid out for my podcast for the next six months? Check!

I was going to get organized, study, create—even start this book—as I *thrived* my way into the new year!

Insert the narrative of that scene from the movie *Father of the Bride Part II* where the main character foreshadows how his life is getting ready to go topsy-turvy: "All those who think they have it made, take one step forward. Not so fast, George Banks."

Not so fast, Christy Nockels. Only eight days into 2018, I found myself sitting in an ENT's office while he dropped on me the diagnosis of sudden sensorineural hearing loss. I'd gone in to address what I thought was a possible ear infection, so I didn't bring my husband to the appointment with me. I remember how the doctor's mouth moved as he spoke but I was grasping only about every other word, not because of my hearing loss but because I was in disbelief. I did gather that an MRI might be a good idea to rule out the big stuff that could be causing the hearing loss, like a tumor.

I walked out to my car and sat at my steering wheel with my body sweating, my head spinning, and my eyes filling with tears. I called my husband, Nathan, to try to explain the news, and all I could think of was how many questions I didn't ask the doctor. The MRI, a few days later, produced only more questions as I was told that I'd need to have a neurosurgeon look at a spot on my brain.

So much for all that clear direction on what my year was supposed to look like! Overnight, I had walked straight into one of the biggest health scares of my life. For several weeks, I felt at a total standstill. It was like a part-time job trying to get in to see all the right people and getting all the right people to call me back. I have a whole new compassion for people who are dealing with health issues for themselves or family members. I remember scrolling through Instagram, feeling sidelined while watching everyone else suit up and take the field.

Most afternoons that winter you could find me tucked beneath my bedcovers, watching snow fall outside, while my ears roared with tinnitus. It was borderline maddening, as well as physically and emotionally alarming, to hear this persistent swish and hum in my ears. Yes, this was certainly devastating news for me as a singer. Music is so dear to me that I couldn't even really allow myself to think of what it might mean for the future. Apart from that, though, I realized this was a devastating development for me as a *human*. All kinds of fears surfaced. *Will I always hear this roaring in my ears? Could I lose my hearing completely?* I imagined the loss of so many beautiful sounds that I love: the music of my husband's soothing voice, the harmony that I hear in my children's laughter, and the gentle rush of the wind through the trees that surround our country home.

Yet, as I'll explain in more detail later, God met me here in this big change of plans. I don't know why I didn't see it coming because He's been meeting me like this over and over through the years. For a multitude of reasons that I may never understand, God used the brokenness of my physical ears to compel me to place the ears of my soul against His heart, desperate to truly hear from Him. If I had started that year full speed ahead, with healthy ears, I shudder to think about all that my spiritual ears would have missed out on.

HIS RELENTLESS LOVE

As the Beloved of God, we can be sure that He is relentless in revealing places in our hearts that He's not done fighting for. He loves us that much. When I think about all the hurry-up-and-wait and the things-didn't-go-as-planned seasons of my life, I'm suddenly aware of how those seasons have brought more forward movement and fulfillment than anything else I can remember. I have to believe it's because those seasons drew me back into remembrance not only of *who* I am but, most important, of *whose* I am.

Andrew Murray said,

> Abiding in Him is not a work that we have to do as the condition for enjoying His salvation, but rather a consenting to let Him do all for us, in us, and through us. It is a work He does for us as the fruit and the power of His redeeming love. Our part is simply to yield, to trust, and to wait for what He has promised to perform.[2]

Throughout my life the Lord has shown up in relentlessly loving ways to draw me in and show me who and whose I am. As I share with you some of those stories and the lessons He's instilled, I pray your eyes will be opened to all the relentlessly loving ways that He is coming after *you*.

I had much to own (and still do) in terms of my Belovedness. I've come face to face with the fact that there is an enemy of my soul working hard to keep me from living from my truest self. In fact, you and I both are in the middle of a battle with this enemy. He is relentless in coming against our very identity as the Beloved.[3]

I can't help but think of a home movie from when I was about three years old, singing my favorite song. I was a '70s baby, so this movie is silent. But because I was doing little hand motions to the song, I can tell that it was the first worship song I ever learned, which says, "I'm my Beloved's and He is mine; His banner over me is love." The most endearing thing about the whole picture is that I have a toy rifle strapped around my chest as I'm singing! It makes me giggle because it's such evidence that I was the only girl being raised with all brothers and boy cousins. But recently as I watched it again, I couldn't help but be filled with the truth that worship is a weapon. Worship is simply our response to God, and learning to live as the Beloved is a beautiful response. It's always our best defense against a soul-killing, identity-stealing enemy. And once we start to live from our own Belovedness, we begin to fight on behalf of others so that they can live and rest in it too!

Beloved, hear me fighting for you when I say God's banner over you is love! In fact, I believe that He's calling you to come and rest and *live* underneath that banner even now. You and I actually have a real-life mediator who is here to help us get to the heart of the matter.[4] His name is Jesus. He was the first one to be called Beloved by His Father, and we have been called by His name.

Jesus consistently asked prodding and challenging questions when He walked this earth. In fact, when He met some of His first disciples—as He noticed them following Him one day along the road—He turned and asked, "What do you want?" It sounds a bit abrupt but, at the same time, stunningly bracing in the best way. People who ask these kinds of questions have likely discovered the answers for themselves, and in Jesus's case, He *is* the answer. I also think He knew that some of life's best answers are questions. "Where are you staying?" they asked Him.

He replied, "Come and see."[5]

Beloved, I believe that this invitation is extended to us. To *you.*

Will you heed His call to come and see? To discover who you really are and what you're truly longing for?

FOR REFLECTION OR DISCUSSION

1. Without referring to any milestones, vocations, or achievements, how would you describe the life you long for?

_____

_____

_____

_____

2. In what ways does our culture—even at times Christian culture—give us conflicting messages about the following:

• rest and achievement?

_____

_____

_____

_____

• building community and not being overscheduled?

_____

_____

_____

_____

• following our dreams and being present in the moment?

_____

_____

_____

_____

PART ONE

The Calling of the Beloved

BELOVED, THE HIGHEST CALL ON YOUR LIFE —above any personal passion or pursuit—is to be loved by God and take your place as His child.[1] This means you are to be holy and set apart so that everything you do is done in the name of the Lord Jesus.[2]

This is a *worthy* calling but one that we often don't feel worthy enough to uphold! Because of this, we all have the tendency to labor and strive. Jesus knows this about us, and in His mercy and gentleness, His call to the Beloved rests like a banner over our lives: "Come to me, all who labor and are heavy laden, and I will give you rest. Take my yoke upon you, and learn from me, for I am gentle and lowly in heart, and you will find rest for your souls. For my yoke is easy, and my burden is light."[3]

This call of Jesus is not about a set of rules or

a program to sign up for. He says (and in the original language the "Come" is exclamatory[4]), "Come! Rest in Me." This is a life-changing invitation, especially since He gives us a clear picture here that there *is* work to be done. However, as the Beloved, we've been invited to come and yield ourselves to His "yoke"—where we work from *His* strength, knowing He has already borne the heavy load for those He loves!

2

THE FARM-TABLE EPIPHANY

FIFTEEN YEARS HAVE PASSED, BUT IT FEELS LIKE ONLY yesterday that I sat in silence at my farm table, the humble and familiar center of my mundane. The kids were napping. I had just been cleaning their bathroom, swishing the brush around in the toilet bowl, when a strange sensation shot through my heart of hearts. Something I hadn't experienced in a really long time. The only word that comes to mind to describe it is *contentment*. This feeling was so peculiar to me that I needed to sit down at the table for a minute to process it.

To be honest, contentment felt utterly foreign to me in that season of life. My husband, Nathan, and I were spread thin, as we were at the height of our career in songwriting, recording, and touring nationwide as a Christian music duo called Watermark. It was work we loved, with people we loved, but we were constantly torn up inside by how the demands of our career pulled us away from the most important people in our lives—our children. So this soul-settling peace coming over me while cleaning a toilet was kind of a lot to take in.

That said, I'm guessing that experiencing joy and fulfillment right in the middle of one of the most menial tasks of the day would leave an impression on you too, no matter the season. Having a deep sense that you're somehow right where you're supposed to be is always a welcome surprise, but what about an epiphany at your kitchen table, or wherever you're sitting even now, that could reorient your heart?

For whatever reason, I remember that cleaning the kids' bathroom was an extra big job that day. My five-year-old son was well past potty training, but if you're a boy mom, you know the drill. For a while, you aren't just cleaning the toilet bowl but the entire toilet as well as the floor around it and occasionally the shower curtain if it's next to the toilet, as ours was. I don't recall my train of thought that day in the bathroom. Maybe it was my son's failure to hit the bullseye that got me thinking. Whatever the reason, suddenly in my mind's eye was a picture of a bullseye, just like the one that my friend Lauren had described to me several months earlier, not long after we had first met.

I had been leading worship at an event we both attended in Texas. She approached me afterward with a big hug and said, "I know this might sound strange, but while you were leading worship tonight, I kept seeing concentric circles every time I closed my eyes." I looked at her, super puzzled as she continued. "It was like a Target sign. You know, like a bullseye and then two outer rings." She added that Philippians 2 had kept coming to her mind, and she challenged me to ask God about it in the coming days and weeks.

Now that I know Lauren so well, it doesn't even faze me that she received this picture from the Lord on my behalf. She is such a beautiful mix of whimsy and wisdom beyond her years, and I completely trust that she seeks the heart of God. Matthew 7:17 says, "Every good tree bears good fruit,"[1] and well, even this book is some of the sweet fruit that has come from her words of encouragement that night. But at the time, I admit, it seemed kind of out there.

So there I sat at my table, months later, convinced that God was near and inviting me to something through this strange sense of contentment. I reached for my Bible, and it fell open to a sweet and familiar passage: Psalm 37. In fact, Psalm 37:5 was the scripture God used when He first called me to come to Him as a little girl.

Every day, on the way to my childhood bedroom, I passed a set of plaques hanging in the hallway of our home. Each plaque featured the name of a family member, along with the meaning of their name and a scripture underneath. Mine said, "Christy—Follower of Christ." Printed below that was Psalm 37:5 in the King James Version: "Commit thy way unto the LORD; trust also in him; and he shall bring it to pass." As a child, I let that little wall plaque *name* me, in a way. I didn't understand what being a follower of Christ really meant, but seeing it printed there next to my name, it felt important, essential even. I memorized the verse and learned to handwrite it and wrote it on everything.

My dad has been a pastor my whole life. One Sunday night while he was preaching, I printed that verse out in my very best, seven-year-old penmanship and handed it to my mom, who was sitting beside me. I'll never forget how she took that little piece of paper, which I still have to this day, and turned it over to write a message back to me. She wrote, "Yes, if Christy gives her heart to Jesus, He will show her the way to go." I took her word for it that night. That's the beauty of parenting and mentoring. Until children learn to fully take God at His Word on their own, our words can keep pointing to *His.* I'm ever grateful that my mother's words did just that, like the North Star, guiding me home.

I remember looking down the long aisle of pews as my dad beckoned anyone who'd like to put their trust in Christ to come forward. With sweaty palms and my little heart beating wildly, I stepped out and walked down in front of our congregation. I reached for my earthly father's hand as I embraced my heavenly Father's heart for me. I wholeheartedly believe that Jesus whispered my heart awake that night and that I received, right then and there, the first and highest calling on my life: to be a Beloved child of God.

Years later, there at my farm table, God brought to my remembrance my gospel story. The moment that I was reconciled to Him and this Abba cry—a heart bellow set deep within me by the Spirit of God, assuring me of whom I belong to—was first awakened in my heart.[2] He was pointing me back to both the simplicity and the significance and, yes, the power of being His Beloved child. As I read Psalm 37 and came to verse 4 that day, it was like I was reading it for the very first time. I'll admit, the weight of it surprised me a little because it's one of those verses that gets printed on tea towels and coffee cups. You probably could say it by memory even now: "Take delight in the LORD, and he will give you your heart's desires."[3] To be really honest, for much of my life I had read this passage to sort of mean that if I scratched God's back, He'd scratch mine. Or, maybe it was something like if I busied myself doing things for God, maybe He'd be proud of me and throw me a bone here and there. Sadly, figuring out how to delight myself in the Lord seemed like a means to an end. If I would give Him what He wanted, maybe He'd return the favor.

Somehow, in the years since I had first heard God name me His Beloved, that first and highest calling had become more of a duty to uphold than a cherished identity. I can't tell you how grateful I am that God fights for places in our hearts that we've either given up on or don't even know need rescuing. Right there in my kitchen, He was fighting for me as He began to speak to me through His Word opened before me: *Just enjoy Me.* He didn't speak audibly, but my heart filled with a knowing that it was Him. It had been a long while since I had heard Him speak so clearly and plainly, and the certainty of His presence unraveled me. It had also been a long time since I had truly enjoyed God. I loved Him, no doubt. I worshipped Him and made Him known to the world with my songwriting and artistry. But enjoying Him? I am not even sure I knew how to do it at that point in my life, nor did I feel that I had the space for it.

It was as if the Lord was pressing into my heart in that moment and showing me what was valuable to Him. It felt like He was nudging my spirit awake again. I'm grateful beyond words that God came in and valued Himself on my behalf when I had clearly forgotten how to value Him above all things. He opened my eyes again to His intrinsic worth and reminded me that He is in fact the treasure of this life and He is worth being enjoyed. Psalm 63:3 says that His "steadfast love is *better* than life."

HEART'S DESIRE

The drawbridge of my heart slowly began to lower as He spoke again: *Just enjoy Me and I will give you the desires of your heart.* That word *give* seemed to jump off the page. I could see this twofold meaning for the first time. I didn't have language for it in the moment, and the best I know how to describe it even now is that God will both set new desires in us and fulfill deep longings that have always been there.

I've heard it said that He is both the *instiller* and *fulfiller* of our desires and longings. I only recently discovered that the Hebrew word for "give" in this passage is *nathan*. First of all, I love God's kindness and attention to detail that He'd set my husband's name, Nathan, right in the middle of what I consider to be my life's passage of Scripture! This word *nathan* means "to give, put, set."[4] So part of what God is saying here is that He will put new desires in us, as in He will show us what our desires are. This isn't some puppet-on-a-string kind of thing. I believe that this is God teaching us to dream bigger in terms of what we long for, to be open to God-sized things in our lives. I believe He's also saying that part of the blessing in learning to enjoy Him is that our hearts' desires will be fulfilled. I would experience both of these things firsthand in that season—that He dreams much bigger dreams for us than we even know how to dream for ourselves and that He Himself satisfies more than any dream fulfilled ever could.

I read on to the verse that changed my life so long ago: "Commit everything you do to the LORD. Trust him, and he will help you."[5] I realized that I hadn't ever really focused much on the rest of the passage. I was intrigued, as I read on, to learn how He would help me. Verse 6 says, "He will make your innocence radiate like the dawn, and the justice of your cause will shine like the noonday sun." As clear as day, He spoke again, pressing these words into my heart: *Do you trust Me with your cause?* My heart, now tender to the touch, wanted to trust Him with my cause, but I also wanted to understand what in the world He was asking of me!

I believe that God's question to me about my cause that day was also twofold.

The word translated as "innocence" in verse 6 can also be translated as "righteousness" or "rightness." I see it so clearly now. He was asking, *Do you trust Me with your righteousness?* As in *Are you willing to rest in Jesus as your righteousness, or are you going to keep exhausting yourself trying to come up with your own?* This was a valid question, as God knew that at that point in my life, doing good things for Him was what made me feel most validated and *right* before Him and even others. The Bible likens this sort of self-righteousness to "filthy rags."[6] God was bringing me face to face with my gospel story again. He wanted me to remember that Jesus alone is my "rightness." Not only had He come to save me; He had come to restore me to Himself so that I might live from who He is.

The second crucial part of God's question to me was this: *Do you trust Me with your dreams, with your longings, with your reputation, and with what you feel called to do? Do you trust Me with the life you want and even long for?* The cause He asked me to entrust to Him I believe also represented my own wants and dreams, things I wanted to promote and prosper in and even win at. He met me right where I was—as He meets all of us right where we are today, asking if we are willing to place our gifts, our talents, our passions, and the very cause we hold dear completely in His hands.

As I considered His invitation to trust, this is when the tears showed up. Unknowingly, I had made my reputation and my platform—using my gifts, talents, and passions for God—the center of my whole world. After all, He had given me these gifts. Surely it was my responsibility to manage them and use them to make Him known to the world!

As I sat with these monumental truths, it was as if those concentric circles that Lauren had described were drawn right there on the pages of Scripture in front of me. The Word of God, living and active, was bringing context to this bullseye picture that had come to my mind while cleaning the toilet.

The Lord has brought more clarity and definition to this over the years since, but even then I sensed that the outermost circle represented my cause—my achievements, my dreams and wants, and the endless to-do list that goes along with all that. The circle just inside that represented my relationships—my marriage, my children, my family and friends, my church, and our ministry partners and community. And the bullseye, the calm at the center of it all, represented God's heart, where I found my place as His Beloved.

I saw myself stuck in that outermost ring, racing in circles, exhausted, determined to prove to God and others my worth and devotion. In this outside-in way of living, I hit the ground running every morning. The to-do list took precedence over my soul needs as I focused tenaciously on doing everything I thought I was supposed to be doing for God and even for myself so life would go as planned. My spirit grieved as I realized that I had assumed I couldn't afford the luxury of spending time with God. I had believed the lie that I had far too many important responsibilities to spend time being still before Him. When I did make time for Him, in exhaustion, my priority was to ask Him to help me with everything that I had spinning: motherhood, home keeping, career building. With a twinge of shame always lingering in my gut, I'd ask His forgiveness for failing to give Him more. Yet I had no more to give because my own strength was gone.

Don't get me wrong. I longed to simply be still. I craved margin and rest and the capacity to put my family first. But I felt trapped in this outer ring, fearful that if I said no to anything, I might miss out on the Next. Big. Thing. Because I would *yes* myself into more than I could handle, I didn't have the capacity to truly see others around me. I was usually in such a frazzled state that I valued community primarily for what it could do for me. For lack of a better word, this is *hustling,* and I've learned that God doesn't always intervene right away when we strive at this kind of pace. Sometimes He gives us what we think we want so that we will finally discover what we truly need. Eventually, though, because He loves us, He will let us feel the weight of trying to call all the shots and do all the things. This was certainly one of those moments in my life.

God's kindness to me that day at my farm table led me to repentance. It was as if He was holding me together while I fell apart right there in my kitchen. I realized I had ditched the first and highest calling on my life as a loved child of God. My heart was broken that singing for God had somehow become more important to me than sitting with Him. I had been busy holding up a cause cloaked in broken strategies, trying to ensure my calling unfolded as I expected. Consumed by a determination to keep up with the world around me, fearful of being left in the dust, I had stopped trusting my Father. I had lost my first love. As my tears poured out onto the pages of Scripture in front of me, God spoke the most life-giving and life-saving words to me: *Just hit the bullseye, and I will take care of all the outer rings of your life. I will hold up your cause and show you My glory.*

THE LIE OF THE ENEMY—AND THE TRUTH THAT SETS US FREE

I feel pretty vulnerable sharing this part of my story with you. I wish we were sitting together over coffee so I could maybe see you nod your head a few times along the way, signaling that my experience resonates with your own. Even without that connection, though, I feel certain you can relate to my struggle. We are all prone to outside-in living and outer-ring hustling because our tendency to make a way for ourselves goes all the way back to the Garden of Eden. Our fear of trusting God is universal. Rather than stepping into His invitation to live from His best, we settle for what we can make happen on our own.

I'm guessing that you, too, long for contentment and rest. But the culture we live in demands that we maintain a certain pace. For many of us, living through a quarantine in the middle of a worldwide pandemic revealed just how much we've leaned into that pace, relied on that pace, and even compromised in the deepest part of our souls because of it. Perhaps, like many others, you've recognized the consequences of those compromises and you don't ever want to go back to the way things were.

Yet even when circumstances all but demand a pause, you and I are told nonstop by this world—and by what we scroll through nonstop—that no one is going to get our dream done for us. We've got to get out there and make it happen! So with clenched teeth, we try to keep up, driven to uphold our family, our dreams, our career, and our reputation. The pressure is often so fierce that we don't even know how to pause and assess where we really are.

To top it all off, the Enemy of our souls is working overtime to keep us from living from our truest selves. Sometimes his deceptive plot comes packaged in the subtlest of lies. One of his most venomous whispers in my own life sounds like this: *It's all up to you.* I wonder if you've heard this one too? This lie is the antithesis of the life that God offers us. And yet we might agree with this lie without even knowing it. Even as we live out what we think is our calling, this lie heaps all the weight and worry of the outcome on our own shoulders. It places all the responsibility on our performance and our own ability to make a way for ourselves in this world. It's eventually destructive as it feeds our tendency toward self-sufficiency. I realize that you may have been taught from infancy that self-reliance is the key to making it in this life. But as we'll learn later, our own sufficiency has a shelf life. Some of us expire faster than others, but eventually, we are all going to fizzle out at this kind of pace. And the repercussions can be devastating.

Often our Enemy's fiercest strategy against us as the Beloved is keeping us consumed with living *for* God rather than living *from* God. Our Enemy knows full well that when we live *from* God, it lifts the burden and the stress and the striving and restores to us the joy of knowing God and loving Him. This joy is contagious! Living from the bullseye of our Belovedness, we begin to trust God alone with what makes us right before Him and with this cause that we hold so dear. After all, He said if we would commit everything we do to Him, He would help us! If we will find our joy in Him, He will be the one to fulfill our deepest desires. And as we spend time enjoying Him, His Word says that His presence makes us "full of gladness."[7]

Please hear me out. This is not some kind of karma version of following Christ. I'm not suggesting that if we follow God, He will make everything turn out magical for us. Being God's Beloved does not make us immune to walking through deep pain and even tragedy in this life. We still live in a broken world, and Jesus Himself told us that we will have trouble in this life. But in the same breath He said, "Take heart; I have overcome the world."[8] As the Beloved of God, we get to draw near to this Jesus who has already overcome this world we're trying so desperately to survive in!

It takes me back to the overarching theme of Psalm 37: that we don't have to fret when we see the world's system—as godless as it is—prospering as well as promoting and even winning at what looks like success. God's promise to His people here is that in time, He will make a clear distinction between the world's system and His economy, between those who trust in mere humans and those who choose to trust in the Overcomer of this world![9]

Learning to trust God with my cause and live from my Belovedness has not happened overnight. Mine was a slow surrender, and still to this day, I have to pause often in a week's time to recenter my heart in God's truth. You'll see in the pages to come that I'm still a work in progress when it comes to trusting that my rightness before God (and others) is in Christ alone. You'll hear about how I've had to learn to lay down my cause for His, surrendering my own wants and desires for the more that He's always had in His heart for me. I still have to choose to trust God before my feet even hit the floor in the mornings, to remember that He sees me, hears me, knows me, and loves me. To ask Him to help me resist the tendency to hustle to the outer ring and instead rest in who He is and who I am in Him so that I can fully blossom in what it looks like to follow Him and show His love to the world around me.

Living like this positions us to approach the outermost rings of our lives with intentionality and purpose. With God holding up our cause, we become available to Him and to others in a way that we never have before.

As I mentioned, God showed me that the next outer ring from the bullseye represented some precious people in my life: my family, my church, my friends, and our ministry partners. You may also remember that Lauren mentioned Philippians 2 to me, just after she told me about the concentric circles she saw in her mind's eye. Part of this passage, which we'll look further into later, says, "Do nothing from selfish ambition or conceit, but in humility count others more significant than yourselves. Let each of you look not only to his own interests, but also to the interests of others."[10]

God was reordering my life to see that I was never meant to go it alone, nor were my own interests ever supposed to be king of my life. In fact, He'd show me that walking arm in arm with my community into the things He's prepared in advance for me is a crucial part of the life that my soul truly aches for.[11]

YOUR PLACE IN HIS HEART

I don't know where all this hits you or where you sit today in your journey of truly trusting God and even enjoying Him in this life. I do know this: there is a place for you in His heart as well as a place for Him in yours. Jesus said in John 14:23, "If anyone loves me, he will keep my word, and my Father will love him, and we will come to him and make our *home* with him."

Regardless of what you might think, God loves you, Beloved. You know what else? He's not far from you, He's not mad at you, and He's made a way for you to come be near Him. Even if you feel far from Him, maybe even stuck in the outer ring and prone to outside-in living, He has not deserted you or given up on you. *He is right there with you,* lovingly calling you back to the center of who He is.

Psalm 145:18 says, "The LORD is near to all who call on him, to all who call on him in truth." Right where you sit, you can call on Him even now, surrendering your life to come and live as His Beloved child. It doesn't have to be an eloquent prayer. I've seen Him work wonders with "God, if You're real, show me."

Here in this purest place at the center of His heart, in accepting this beautiful invitation to inside-out living, you will truly rest and find contentment. And, Beloved, when you begin to live wholly out from His love, you will see Him show up on your behalf as you never have before.

FOR REFLECTION OR DISCUSSION

1. In what ways, if any, have you felt your highest calling was "more of a duty to uphold than a cherished identity" (page 21)? How has this been reflected in your relationship with God?

_____

_____

_____

_____

2. What is your first reaction to the idea of "enjoying" God? What might that look like for you?

_____

_____

_____

3. In what part of your life right now—such as work, family, ministry—are you most likely to feel it's all up to you?

_____

_____

_____

_____

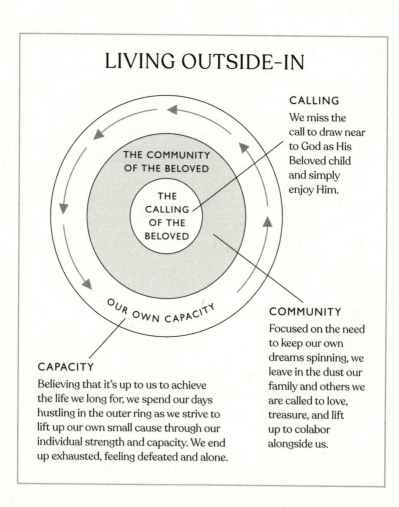

LIVING OUTSIDE-IN

THE COMMUNITY OF THE BELOVED

THE CALLING OF THE BELOVED

OUR OWN CAPACITY

CALLING
We miss the call to draw near to God as His Beloved child and simply enjoy Him.

COMMUNITY
Focused on the need to keep our own dreams spinning, we leave in the dust our family and others we are called to love, treasure, and lift up to colabor alongside us.

CAPACITY
Believing that it's up to us to achieve the life we long for, we spend our days hustling in the outer ring as we strive to lift up our own small cause through our individual strength and capacity. We end up exhausted, feeling defeated and alone.

LIVING INSIDE-OUT

CALLING

We start each day from our place in God's heart as His Beloved child. We live out our gospel story allowing Christ's life to live through us as we "re-present" Him to the world.

THE COMMUNITY OF THE BELOVED

THE CALLING OF THE BELOVED

THE CAPACITY OF THE BELOVED

COMMUNITY

We live out from God's love and "see and sing over" those He has placed in our path. We fight for the "Belovedness" of others by welcoming them into our "familiar with the Father."

CAPACITY

We live in our fullest, God-capacity, which is Christ in us, together with the family of God and showing God's love to a barren world.

3

THE GLORIOUS
IN THE MUNDANE

THE WORDS GOD DROPPED INTO MY HEART THAT DAY at the kitchen table—*Just hit the bullseye*—offered a clear and present call to come back to the purest place of living as the Beloved of God. More specifically, it was an invitation to come *home,* spiritually and even physically.

Spiritually, God was beckoning me to draw nearer to Him in the secret place, to experience being His child in a way that I never had before. The call to come home physically started—I kid you not—with swishing the toilet bowl clean that day. I like to think it was God's way of showing me that contentment could show up in the places I least expected. I believe that He was inviting me to come and practice living from the supernatural. I'm not talking about some kind of weird paranormal stuff. The supernatural life God offers us is one of rest and trust and watching Him come through when we rest and trust in Him. This call was to come and experience how valuing Him and prioritizing His promises and principles—and my own soul in the process—could produce something unexpectedly life changing.

The contentment that flooded in that day met me with a readied heart. Who knew that a readied heart could look like a frazzled and weary heart? Who knew that God ushering in His dreams for us could look like our own plans being thwarted or even just our desires beginning to unexpectedly shift?

In the year or two leading up to my farm-table epiphany, Nathan and I had been living in the uneasy tension that something had to give. Even though we were intentional about spending our lives on good things, our professional schedules were so full that our personal lives, mainly our family life, was being suffocated. As you know, in the world you and I live in, quitting something feels like an unrealistic luxury. Irresponsible even. We were tied to a recording contract as well as a partnership with a management company and a booking agency. So when we started saying no to a few things here and there out of protection of our little family, we began to feel some pushback. We wrestled, holding both sides of the tension. We felt strongly that God was asking us to reprioritize our lives, but we also knew that all these well-meaning people had businesses to run and jobs to do.

Soon after we took steps to lighten our load, our manager at the time came by our house to deliver the news from the higher-ups that they would be dropping Nathan and me from their roster. Our dream of putting our family first was apparently not a shared dream, and that's okay. I see it much clearer now than I did then.

But on that day, we sat in our den, trying to wrap our minds around the news, grappling to understand the resistance to our efforts at finding a healthy balance for our family. For a little bit of context, I was neck deep in postpartum *everything* from the birth of our second child, so the news hit a little too close to home. Normally, I might have just listened in silence, but all the mama in me rose up to defend my roost! Just as I started in on our manager to give him a piece of my mind, I caught Nathan's eye. He shot me a look that said, "It's not worth it. Don't go there." I paused, and just about the time I decided to completely disregard Nathan's leading, the baby monitors lit up with the cries of both of our children waking from their naps at the same time. Knowing that this was my second warning to shut my mouth, I quietly exited the room. Looking back, I love how clearly God highlighted what (and whom) I was supposed to fight for in that moment.

As I lifted our cuddly baby girl from her crib and walked into the hallway, I was met by Nathan holding our toddler son in his arms. There we stood, holding everything that truly mattered in our little world. The locking of our eyes said it all as we envisioned the choices before us, choices that would determine the trajectory of our children's lives. One option was to just keep clinging to the world and its ways of getting things done, which we knew would be at the expense of our family. Or we could choose to step into the mystery of trusting that God would make a way for us if we obeyed what He was pressing into our hearts. Both choices seemed daunting. Really, we were just two kids ourselves who needed parenting by our heavenly Father in that moment. Even then, God was pointing us to the bullseye and what it might look

like to crawl up underneath His care and trust Him to provide a way for us in this life.

Nathan asked what I was thinking. I remember saying, "I
have an overwhelming sense that God will take care of us no
matter what."

Realizing our guest had left, I asked if anything more had
been said after I'd left the room. Nathan said, "No more
words were spoken. I just walked him to the door."

Perplexed that this surreal scenario was playing out, I said,
"Wow, that's awkward. What are *you* thinking?"

In true Nathan form, quiet and collected, he said, "All I
could think on the way to the door was . . . *Get off my land
and don't touch my roosters!*" Realizing that he was serious made
me love him all the more, but it also got me giggling. Soon
our shared laughter broke through the tension. We didn't
have any roosters, of course. This was just all the daddy rising
up in Nathan to defend the treasure of his home.

As you can see, the moment at the farm table was this
beautiful culmination of God having prepared me to step into
the mystery with Him by allowing my heart to become both
fatigued and dissatisfied with life as I knew it. Had I chosen
to stay out in the peripheral facets of my life and calling, I
have no doubt I would have still done good things *for* God.
But in answering this call to come home to the purest place
of living my life *from* Him, I experienced transformation like
I'd never known, from the inside out. A contentment that
would eventually lead to contending for kingdom things as I
never had before.

God's invitation to the bullseye marked the start of my
learning how to be surrendered. He was calling me to come

and lay everything down: my gifts, my talents, and everything that I was so busy doing for Him. But it actually took me a minute—more like a few months—to realize that He was asking me to *literally* come home, as in lay down my career. He was calling me to come and rest. I know this may ruffle some feathers—trust me, it ruffled mine! God was asking me not only to value Him and this home that He has made for Himself in my heart but also to value my actual home here on earth—my husband and my children. Even though what He asked of me felt enormous in terms of what I was laying down, there was also something simple about the call that kept singing to my heart. It seemed that everywhere I turned in that season, God was using the sights and sounds around me to bid me to come and *be* His child, to enjoy Him and learn to live my life *from* Him. To hit the bullseye every day and to trust Him with all the things that I'd been hustling for.

NOTHING TO OFFER EXCEPT MYSELF

After praying and seeking counsel from trusted pastors and friends, Nathan and I officially decided to go palms up with our career as recording artists. This meant letting go of Watermark, the music career that had been a vital part of our ministry and even our identities for so long. After enduring who-knows-how-many flights with newborns, sleeping in bunks on buses, strapping car seats into cabs, and me nursing my babies in countless janitor closets, our hearts ached for stability and home. Since we'd traveled on weekends for much of our career, we longed to be a part of our church on

Sundays. I started wanting to do strange things (at least in my world) like bake casseroles and take them to friends who had just had babies. I wanted to push our baby girl's stroller through the neighborhood on a weekend while our son learned to ride his bike. I know, those are all very normal things, and that's exactly what we were longing for.

Maybe you know from experience how hard it is to lay down a career or a ministry or something you've worked so hard to build. If so, you know full well that the choice doesn't come without pain and tears—and a belly full of fear. For us, it meant clearing everything from our calendars and starting over in many ways, which was both terrifying and hopeful at the same time.

I'll admit that at first, this call to come home and own my Belovedness wasn't quite as alluring as writing songs and leading worship. For this reason, I believe God spoke specifically through that toilet-cleaning moment to remind me that He could show up in the most mundane moments of my life and fill them with His presence. I didn't have to be leading on a public stage to experience His glory or to sense His nearness. It could happen anytime, anywhere. Of course, hearing this truth proved much easier than remembering it and truly living it, as I would soon discover.

Nathan had a longing to pursue music production, and my coming home would give him the time and space to walk toward that. His production career would eventually grow into an entirely new branch of creativity and, thankfully, income for our little family.

As for my own transition home, I *so* want to tell you that it was seamless and smooth and that I immediately settled into my new normal. It was actually quite the opposite. In fact, I got an immersion course in what it means to truly live from my Belovedness, with nothing to bring to God but myself.

The newness of being home 24/7 quickly wore off, and this road girl had no idea how to cook or clean or take care of a home. Soon, the toilet cleanings were just plain ol' toilet cleanings. I began to battle fear that I would not be able to find purpose in the unseen tasks of motherhood and keeping house. Subconsciously, I still saw my worth as being rooted in what I could *do*. My identity and sense of purpose had somehow become woven into the visibility of my platform. Because of this, I bought into the lie that mundane tasks were an inglorious waste of my time.

While I delighted in Nathan's growing production business, it added to my sense of now feeling swallowed by normalcy. We had built out our basement as a space where he could create and produce albums for other artists. But the way I saw it, every morning he got to skip downstairs and do what he loved while I was upstairs dealing with the everyday stuff of life. Every once in a while, I'd hear the sound of other artists singing and songwriting as it echoed up through the air vents into the humdrum of my day. I'd catch myself feeling anxious all over again about everything that I had just laid down. Too many days of feeling hidden away like this left me convinced that I was missing my calling, which was surely found somewhere other than the four walls of my kitchen!

My head stayed in the clouds, constantly dreaming of creative endeavors beyond the borders of my home. All the while, our fridge was full of rotting food that I wouldn't take the time to get creative with. I was too busy worrying and even sulking about my transition from leading worship in arenas to watching reruns of *Blue's Clues.* I look back on so many rushed-through moments with the kids and days that felt purposeless simply because of my own lack of purpose. I might have physically come home in that season, but spiritually I had reverted to outer-ring living, even from my own living room! But God was so faithful to keep calling my heart back to His.

One day a songwriter who came to work with Nathan asked if I would sing a demo for a song she had written. Excited to do anything pertaining to music, I skipped down the stairs *with* Nathan that morning. And because God dreams bigger dreams than we can ever dream for ourselves (and also has an interesting way of unfolding those dreams), my meeting Teri that morning was about so much more than music. This beautiful lady immediately reminded me of Jesus, and this drew me to her. I was also intrigued by the fact that she was a songwriter, a blogger, and a mother who homeschooled her *nine* children!

A few weeks later, I sat across from Teri in the middle of a coffee shop, with tears in my eyes, and asked how in the world she did it all. I guess I was expecting a pep talk or a step-by-step program on life management. You know, I thought this amazing woman was going to give me the secret 411 on somehow living the balanced life in the middle of my mother load.

So I was a little taken aback when Teri's eyes welled up with tears as well. I realize now that she was still very much in the thick of it all herself. She looked at me, and her words (which I believe were the Holy Spirit's words to me) went right through me: "You invite the *glorious* into the mundane." I sat there stunned. It was so not what I expected, and it definitely wasn't what I wanted to hear. I needed the program. You know, the chart with boxes to check that I could hang on my laundry room wall. I needed something to *do* because that's how I felt most productive and purposeful and even loved. Yet here it was again—this invitation to mystery.

A HEART IN HIS HANDS

If you're sitting there sweating and concluding that to live in the bullseye of your Belovedness, God is going to ask you to lay down all your dreams—including your career—hear this, Beloved: God is coming after your heart. Of all the things He wants you to lay down, *you* are the most important to Him. For me, God happened to specifically use the struggle of laying down my career and embracing motherhood to posture my heart in surrender. I imagine that God uses an infinite number of ways to replace our hustle obsession with His grander desires for us as His children.

You might have just embarked upon marriage or a new job or a fresh start in a new town, and as exciting as it all is, maybe it has stirred feelings of inadequacy and unrest or even a sense of being overwhelmed by change. Maybe you are single and the years that you envisioned yourself "thirty, flirty and thriving"[1] have turned out a bit more like you hunkering down for survival in what feels like the wild, wild West. Your tension might be that you're weighted down by loads of pressure in having to work full time just to make it. So this call to come home and rest might feel completely out of reach for you. Or maybe you're on the brink of surrendering something you have felt God asking you to release but you're paralyzed in fear of what it might look like to trust that He's really going to come through for you on the other side.

Again, more than anything you could be doing right now with your life, God is all about who you are becoming. Even in the midst of your most difficult circumstances and some of the most complicated plotlines of your story, there is always a bigger invitation from Him and a deeper ask. He's calling you to come home to His heart. He might propose that you surrender and lay down some things in your life, but ultimately the question He's really asking is this: "Do I have your whole heart?"

Why would He want your whole heart? Because He knows what can be entrusted to a fully surrendered heart. This is why we're called to prioritize His promises and His principles. When we do, we begin to see that His way works. Second Chronicles 16:9 says, "The eyes of the LORD run to and fro throughout the whole earth, to give strong support to those whose heart is blameless [or whole, as the footnote says] toward him." Imagine that! A heart that is wholly turned toward God is met by God Himself already looking for ways that He can show Himself strong to you! God knows and trusts His own strength, so wouldn't it be like Him to entrust and empower a heart completely yielded to Him?

I've shared with you all this stuff from my past, some so embarrassing to admit, not just to air a bunch of dirty laundry. My intent is to show you the condition my heart was in, even as someone who professed Christ. Even as someone in ministry, deeply devoted to making God known and living for Him.

I wonder if you can relate to trudging and limping through the Christian life? Where we take on the enormous task of living for God all on our own, only to fail in our frailty over and over again. Where we tend to just keep picking ourselves up by our Chelsea boots and going about our hustle, never making the margin to stop and ask whether there's more. Where we struggle to keep up with a world that we weren't even made for, desperately trying to survive at a pace that we were never meant to run in. We strive for fulfillment and pine for contentment. But what if our striving and pining are preventing the supernatural work of God in our lives? *What if our hustling is actually holding us back?*

Beloved, I can promise you this: what God actually requires of you today is a welcomed relief in comparison to all that you are trying to carry on your own. Think about it: if there's a hustle that holds us back, wouldn't it be like God to provide a rest that actually propels us? Isn't it just like Him to give us a surrender that looks more like a superpower? Isn't it just His way to give us the highest calling on our lives of becoming His children?

OUR HOPE OF GLORY

I look back now with such a sense of gratitude and awe that God would call me home to raise my children. That He would so intentionally cause my heart to turn toward my little ones as a way of pointing me—every day—to the one thing He truly desires from me: to be His loved child and to live from that humble and trusting posture.

I can't help but think about when Jesus's disciples asked Him, "Who is the greatest in the kingdom of heaven?" Jesus called a child to come over, and He placed the child in the middle of everyone and said, "Truly, I say to you, unless you turn and become like children, you will never enter the kingdom of heaven. Whoever humbles himself like this child is the greatest in the kingdom of heaven."[2]

Jesus essentially laid out the qualifications for being the greatest in the kingdom of God, and it was to become like a *child?* I can't tell you how much I love that my study Bible says this in the notes next to this very passage: "The humility of a child consists of childlike trust, vulnerability, and the inability to advance his or her own cause apart from the help, direction, and resources of a parent."[3] If I could use the loudly crying face emoji here, I would! Do you know how much energy I've wasted in trying to hold up and advance my own cause? Whether it was toiling to ensure that my dreams would be realized or approaching God over and over with the rags of my own self-righteousness, I was trusting in my own resources and looking out for me and only me.

Imagine the deep soul rest that comes to our hearts when we surrender our *all* and behold this Father who already has His eyes on us! The One who placed all these gifts and talents and dreams in us—wouldn't He be the best promoter of our cause that ever existed?

The highest calling on your life, to be the Beloved child of God, simply requires your surrender today. In surrender, you are saying that you believe that from Him you can do all things and without Him you can do nothing.[4] Trust me, if you choose this one thing—*surrender to God*—the supernatural will show up and surprise you! When you lay down your life, you will truly find it.[5]

The most beautiful part of trusting in God as your provider and your promoter is that, not only do you walk into dreams that He's already prepared in advance for you, but you also begin to experience a satisfaction in His love that none of your previous wants and desires or dreams could ever come close to fulfilling. You become transformed from the inside out. In fact, your cause begins to look like His cause: your surrendered life proclaiming Christ. Paul passed on this commission to us, describing it as "the riches of the glory of this mystery, which is *Christ in you,* the hope of glory."[6]

Beloved, the first step toward living from God's love is to accept the way that He has already loved you—by receiving the gift of His Son, Jesus. Not just for salvation but as your strength, life, and sufficiency every morning when you look in the mirror, acknowledging that the life of Christ *in* you is how you live *from* the love of God each day. In surrender, we get to partake of living from His glorious life. Galatians 2:20 says, "I have been crucified with Christ. It is no longer I who live, but Christ who lives in me. And the life I now live in the flesh I live by faith in the Son of God, who loved me and gave himself for me."

If you're like me and you've heard this scripture countless times, perhaps your heart has grown numb, conditioned to hearing God's Word but not fully grasping the power that is available to us through it. We profess that we believe in Christ and that we want to live for Him, but let's be honest: it's a whole other thing to be willing to die to ourselves (believing the old self was crucified with Him) so Christ can come and live His life in us and through us. And yet this is the only way that the Christian life is even possible.

Beloved, we were never meant to live the Christian life. Christ has come that He might live it *through* us. Our faith has a resting place, and His name is Jesus! I love how Hudson Taylor, the great missionary to China, described our life in Christ as "the exchanged life."[7] These words were inspired by Isaiah 40:31, another scripture you might know well: "They who wait for the LORD shall renew their strength; they shall mount up with wings like eagles; they shall run and not be weary; they shall walk and not faint." The word *renew* in the original language means "pass through, change, substitute."[8] As we look eagerly to Jesus, He exchanges our fragile human strength for His matchless strength!

Christ in you is your blessed assurance on that final day when He returns, but it is just as much your blessed assurance today in the carpool line or at the checkout counter at the grocery store or in folding that endless pile of laundry. It's your gospel story lived out all day long, breathing in the truth that it's *not* all up to you today.

Bullseye living is a continual surrender to God, with the power of Christ living in you and through you! We will talk about this more later, but it transforms the way that you see God every day, the way that you see yourself, and the way that you see others. It's how I can hug the neck of that manager every time I see him around town now—you know, the one who dropped the dreadful news on us that day, which was not-so-dreadful news after all but a beautiful invitation.

What's also beautiful is that I don't see the hustle in his eyes anymore but far more humility and rest. I hope that he sees the same in me. There sure seems to be an unspoken joy when he hears the updates on how God keeps making a way for us to live out the dream of that family-first agenda. What's more, I occasionally even hear about some of those higher-ups around town and catch wind of how they are loving and leading people well.

It's amazing how when we begin to live as the Beloved of God, we start to see it in others and desire it for them. People become treasured far above the pace, above an industry and a mentality and a culture, and we learn to love each other as loved people do. Even when there isn't a neatly tied bow or a happy ending on a fallout with others, a surrendered heart learns to forgive and keep hope alive for restoration yet to come.

Living loved turns our mundane into a place of glorious encounters with this God who is already on the edge of His seat, looking for a heart that might turn toward Him today. This posture of surrender transfers our trust from mere humans making a way for ourselves to the God of the universe showing Himself strong to us. This sets us up to receive the blessings that He gives those who trust in Him—not earthly treasures or a magical, perfect life but the kind of blessings that make our lives look like "a tree planted by streams of water, which yields its fruit in season and whose leaf does not wither."[9]

Christ in you, Beloved. It's the hope that you can cling to today for the life you're longing for. That living from God's love is not only possible but is what you were created for. *It is the rest that propels you.* The chance to live out in real time what it looks like to trust God with every season and every sunrise.

FOR REFLECTION OR DISCUSSION

1. Why do you think it's so tempting to find our identities in what we do rather than in who we are?

   _____

   _____

   _____

   _____

2. Consider this statement: "What God actually requires of you today is a welcomed relief in comparison to all that you are trying to carry on your own" (page 44). Do you agree or disagree, and why?

   _____

   _____

   _____

   _____

3. What would you identify as the key difference(s) between our living Christian lives and Christ living through us?

   _____

   _____

   _____

   _____

4

THE ALREADY OF OUR STORY

ALONG MY JOURNEY TOWARD UNDERSTANDING MY Belovedness and how to live from it, I acquired an unlikely mentor. In fact, if you had told me when I was a teenager that my older brother Eric would disciple me in my thirties, I most certainly would have laughed out loud!

There were three of us kids. Our oldest brother, Shaun, was out of the house and married before I even clued in to the fact that my family members were *real* people—with stories, feelings, and journeys all their own. Eric took up his middle-child space with flying colors. I was the youngest and the only girl. The two of us were closer in age, so that meant we were both still in the house together a bit longer.

We shared a love for music, and he introduced me to all the great bands and songwriters of the '80s and '90s, which led to him inspiring much of my own songwriting and even our cowriting some songs together through the years.

Our dad pastored a big church in a small town, which means we were raised in that whole fishbowl dynamic, where it often felt like people were looking in on us with furrowed brows. That probably wasn't the case, at least most of the time, but that fishbowl often felt more like a pressure cooker with no way to let out any steam.

Somehow, long before Eric's heart began to turn toward the Lord, I *saw* it there. I held out hope for a lot of years that all that wildness and fire would one day embody the heart of Jesus, and it has. Eric grew from a rebellious, lost boy to one of the most cherished voices in my walk with Jesus.

One afternoon several years after my farm-table epiphany, Eric called to ask if I'd be his guinea pig for some content that the Lord had put on his heart. He and his wife, Kristin, were starting a nonprofit ministry to help others live from a heart of rest. Previously, Eric had spent fifteen years in ministry positions at megachurches where he, too, had struggled with outer-ring living. He would tell you that in those early years of ministry, he might have believed and even taught that Belovedness was possible for others but he had never fully believed it to be true of himself. Rather than stepping into the mystery of trusting God, he settled for the exhaustion of managing life on his own, depending on his own limited commitment and capacity. Now that he'd experienced what it meant to live from rest, he was eager to help others find the same freedom.

I accepted Eric's invitation with joy, thinking that I could be a good sounding board and an encouragement to him. Little did I know, the Lord had in mind to carve out an even deeper space in my heart to live as His Beloved!

We were living states apart at the time, so we settled for a weekly phone call. My house was loud with littles, as Nathan and I now had three arrows in our quiver. The quietest place I could find was my carpeted closet floor. In that season, you could find me lying facedown, in tears many afternoons, on the phone with Eric—marveling that God was calling both of us to discover what it looks like to truly rest. After four years or so of home being my mainstay and God helping me reprioritize my world, I had started songwriting again and leading worship and even traveling a few times here and there. It was a slow emerging as I tried to figure out how to live in my God-propelled capacity from my one true calling of being His Beloved.

Eric had been trained and licensed to walk me through the Birkman Method, a valuable personality assessment, which he planned as my bonus gift for being his guinea pig. However, my brother made it clear that the personality assessment would come at the end of our three-month journey together. He could tell that I was excited to discover more about the way I'm wired, but he explained that while the information I'd learn about myself—what my personality type is, how I relate to people, what I'm like in health and in stress—would be an extremely helpful tool, greater wisdom comes in knowing how to apply this information. He explained that because God is a God of order, it matters where we start when it comes to our identities.

I think you and I would agree that discovering our types and what makes us tick is both fascinating and affirming. There's reassurance in someone's validating how we think and feel and see the world. It can even bring us closer to our Creator as we understand how intricately He has wired each of us. But at the end of the day, I want to find my validation in my Father, not just in how He made me. Long before anyone told me that I was a golden retriever or that my color is blue or that I'm a four, the Spirit of God awakened His Abba cry in me and I became a loved daughter of my glorious Father! This is the *already* of my story that determines my true identity.

And this is where Eric and I started on the phone that day, at the beginning of our beautiful identities—God's covenant love for His own. Yes, we talked about creation and the fall of humankind, but we focused on the already of our story that is the hope you and I rest in today. God is a loving, pursuing God who promised to be *with* us!

We can see it in His covenant with Abraham in Genesis 15 all the way to the new covenant that He established through the sacrifice of His only Son in John 3:16. "For God so loved the world" might culturally have been reduced to bumper stickers and Bible school, but it still declares God's greatest "I will be with you" promise: *Jesus.* And by trusting in Jesus, we get to be in on God's covenant love. In fact, the crowning glory of our gospel story is not necessarily eternal life—although I'm sure we'd all agree that this is wonderful news beyond comprehension!—but the most beautiful part, that you and I are reconciled to God and brought back to His loving arms *even now*. This is where we were always meant to live from. This is where obedience wells up and spills out as we live abundantly from a heart that knows where it belongs.

YOU HAVE WHAT IT TAKES

I recently discovered a tiny Greek word. Just so you know, I'm a bit of a nerd about words. This one might be little, but it packs a serious punch! The word is *ek,* and in Scripture when you see the words *from* God or *of* God or *by* God, they're most likely translated from this mighty little word *ek.* According to HELPS Word-studies, "*ek* ('out of') is one of the most undertranslated (and therefore mistranslated) Greek prepositions—often being confined to the meaning 'by.'" It actually "has a two-layered meaning ('*out from* and *to*') which makes it *out-come* oriented (out of the depths of the source and extending to its impact on the object)."[1]

This goes back to the order of things and how living *out from* God's love propels us from a heart of rest into all that He has ordained and planned for us. As a river flows out from its source and brings refreshment wherever it goes, our lives were made to flow out from God and carry the fullness of His life to everyone around us. When 1 John 4:4 says that we are "from God," it means that we are "out from God and to." To what? Well, there are endless possibilities every day. If you plan to simply go buy groceries today, you are sent *out from* this God who made you and loves you and *to* everyone you will encounter.

In John 20:21 Jesus said, "Peace be with you. As the Father has sent me, even so I am sending you." Isn't it beautiful that like Christ, we are God's representatives? I've seen it said like this: we get to *re-present* Christ to the world![2] Yes, we are His followers, but more than that, His very life gets re-presented through us by the power of His Spirit! What's even more beautiful is to think that you, Beloved, have a unique way that you live out from God to the world around you. When you choose to surrender—to die to yourself and let Christ live His life through you—this doesn't mean that you're just a blob that Christ comes and lives through. This is where Christ comes and expresses His life through your unique and beautiful wiring, which He Himself knit together!

Maybe you relate to a type or a color or a number, but you have an intrinsic worth that extends far beyond being a certain type of person. The truth is, no one has your fingerprints that touch the world the way you do! The way that compassion and kindness shine through your eyes stands alone. Your voice and how it can speak life to your own soul and over the souls around you are unmatched. The way that your heart was made to live out from His is unparalleled. And the cause that keeps you awake at night, the one that God wired into your desires and longings? You are the only one who can surrender it because it's unique to you. And in this surrender, God's heart is not to take it from you, friend. He wants to lift it up for you! He wants to promote you because He had everything to do with fashioning you and He delights in all that He has put in you.

Eric showed me a pattern in Scripture that literally changed the way I read the Bible. Once you see it, you'll notice it all throughout Scripture. Here it is: God most often reminds us of who we are before He asks us to do something. Again, there's an order here that I believe is meant to unlock something really powerful and supernatural in our lives if we let it.

For instance, I don't believe that it was for salutation's sake that Paul in his letter to the Colossians addressed believers in this order: "Therefore, *as God's chosen people, holy and dearly loved,* clothe yourselves with compassion, kindness, humility, gentleness and patience."[3] I can't help but think that this is our Father's loving way of reminding us that our capacity to do what He asks goes all the way back to who we are and whose we are!

As a parent I've come to realize that my children will succeed best in this world if they have a deep understanding of *who* they are. I want them to know deep down that they are sent out from a home where they are seen, known, and loved and that they always have a place to come home to and rest. I want them to know that Nathan and I are with them and for them and that we will help propel them out into this world the best we possibly can.

Even more than that, we want our children to deeply understand *whose* they are. Yes, we want them to know this God that they get to re-present to this world, but most important, we want them to know that it's *out from God* that they will re-present Him. This isn't about them striving to be Christians, nor is it about them managing or mustering up a commitment to make God known. This is about *abiding* in Christ and allowing His Spirit to live through their surrendered hearts. Therefore, by His strength, His capacity, His love, and His *everything,* they will have what it takes!

When our son, Noah, turned eighteen, Nathan and I tried not to panic even as we wondered whether we should make a crash course of everything we wanted him to know before leaving the nest. Not that a song solves everything, but we did write him one. It's called "You Have What It Takes." We choose to trust that if Noah knows who and whose he is, he's going to be okay in this world. Don't get me wrong; it's good to teach our kids how to defend their faith and how to make disciples, but the truth is, faith defending and disciple making will spring up wildly and abundantly when we live from our Belovedness.

Now, if I desire this and believe this on behalf of my own children, how much more does your heavenly Father desire and believe this for you? No wonder He reminds you throughout Scripture of whose you are! The *already* of your story, Beloved, is that you are seen, known, and loved by your Father and you always have a place in Him to come home and rest. He is with you and for you and in you. Through your surrendered heart, He will propel you to do all that He's purposed for you to do. You have what it takes!

THE ORDER OF THINGS

One of the songs that Eric and I cowrote that emerged from our time together in those days is called "Be Loved." I'll never forget his blurting out one day, "You know, it's not until we take our place as the Beloved and allow ourselves to be loved that we can ever truly *be love* to the world around us." We both sat there in the quiet, taking that truth in. I remember wondering, Do we need to acknowledge that, as preacher's kids, we should know these truths already rather than experience them as life-changing epiphanies in spite of their simplicity?

And that was just it. I think the simplicity of it all surprised me the most and kept me in awe. God's ways—His commanded blessings—are designed to propel us into what He has prepared for us. Our surrender to Him and His purposeful order gives God permission to work in our lives in a truly extraordinary way. God specifically chooses to work through our dependency on His Spirit so that even when we are weak, we're strong.[4]

When I heard those words, "take our place as *the Beloved* and . . . *be loved* [before] we can . . . *be love*," not only could I see the order in it all, but I could also visualize the labels on each concentric circle. *Beloved,* of course, is the bullseye of our calling and identity, *be loved* is the middle ring of community, and *be love* is the outermost ring of our capacity. I remember drawing it out on a piece of paper while Eric talked and looking at it as if it were my road map to rest. I became so convicted by God's Spirit all over again of how my habit of hustling had both complicated my life and constricted God's supernatural work in me.

As I looked at that outer ring and stared at those words *be love,* I began to feel tired. I thought about all the times that I had tried and striven to be God's love to the world around me in my own strength rather than intentionally and supernaturally living out from Him. I also thought about how messy it gets when I try to hold up my own cause and be God's love to the world at the same time, all from my own commitment and capacity. It sure does end up being a lot about me, for one thing, but it also gets exhausting. Then, shame rears its ugly head as I sense my love capacity for God and others fading.

This is what it looks like to live outside in. Instead of centering our hearts each day in the bullseye of *who* and *whose* we are, we hustle straight for the outer rings of the *what* and the *why* of our day. When we live from the outside in, we're left pushing in toward God and others from our own capacity. Let me be clear: nothing is wrong with the what and the why of our day or our lives; *it just matters when we get them out of order.*

Most of us don't know when we're in hustle mode, either because it's all we've ever known or because we've hustled for so long that we don't remember how to operate any other way. But maybe you've experienced some of the signs of outer-ring living:

fatigue

overcommitment

fear of failure or missing out

numbness to calling and purpose

depression

isolation from God and others with no desire
    for real community

developing a false sense of community

obsession with social media clout and influence

seeing others as competition and therefore a threat

striving to control your career

attempting to control others

valuing others for what they can do for you

measuring your own worth by what you can do
    for others
moral failure
discouragement
diminishment
deeply questioning your faith, God's love and truth,
    and even His existence

It sounds extreme, but I've lived a lot of these very symptoms. In fact, I come from a family—yes, a pastor's family—that was almost destroyed because of what outer-ring living does to the heart. I believe this is why many Christians have left the faith and even pastors are continually giving up on the Christian life. After trying for years to commit to Christ and do what's right, they simply tucker out.

Instead of being propelled out from the bullseye of our Belovedness, we push and trudge toward God and others from our barrenness. When we attempt to commune with God, our barren hearts cower, certain that He's disappointed in us and He surely doesn't want to be near us. We might spend our time apologizing to Him about our performance and even promising to try harder. With sunken-in hearts, we eventually avoid time with God. We still believe in Him, of course, and want others to be close to Him, but we're too weary and feel too unworthy to make it to the bullseye.

This outside-in order develops in us what I call a commodity mentality, which declares, "I have to be useful to belong." We've essentially adopted the world's system of what it takes to get our needs met and succeed (or be accepted). We value ourselves and assume others value us only for what we can produce, perform, or supply, and all the while we develop the same crooked outlook on others.

The Enemy of the Beloved hates God's gift of community. He seems to do whatever he can to keep it transactional rather than transformational. His strategy is to snuff out God's dream for us to enjoy each other, to fellowship from God's love and even labor together. Think about it: if we define our value by what we do, this leaves us vulnerable to the Enemy to cause all kinds of heartache. When we're not looking to God for our sense of worth, we often look for it in each other. Whether it's two soul-barren people looking for validation and comfort in the arms of each other rather than their spouses or division in the church caused by a spirit of control and wounding words, Satan's aim is to fracture the fellowship of the Beloved.

If you have experienced this kind of hurt or barrenness in the church or in community anywhere, it's important to remember who the real Enemy is. Satan is the one who wants to get you running completely ragged in the outer ring. He wants you angry and alone and hurt and soul barren and burned out. He knows that this kind of diminishment—the feeling that you're just *done*—might snuff out your faith for good.

When we reach the end of our own capacity, we tend to assume the same about God. In our weariness, we project onto God that He, too, is weary and limited, and in our weakness, we humanize Him. We figure that if we don't care anymore, neither does He. We might even start to question whether He's there at all. I've come to believe that the ultimate form of burnout is unbelief.

A COMMANDED BLESSING

Oh, that we might order our lives to rest and begin each day in the bullseye of our Belovedness! As we begin with whose we are and remain alert to the beautiful order woven into Scripture, we'll pay attention when we see a *therefore*. The word is *there for* a reason! What comes after the *therefore* is an extension of what came before it, as if to connect the dots between the two thoughts.

Before the *therefore* in Colossians 3:12, where we read earlier about our role as God's chosen people, you'll find this header over the entire chapter: "Put On the New Self," or as another translation says, "Living as Those Made Alive in Christ."[5] To be clear, living from our Belovedness is just another way to express both of these important commands, lest you think that I believe I've unearthed some sort of new truth. There are no new truths under the sun!

At some point, I began to say "living from my Belovedness" as a synonymous phrase with "putting on the new self" in hopes that the fresh wording would reawaken me to familiar commands in Scripture that had become more like catchphrases than truths to practice and live out. I've learned that some of us are so familiar with Scripture that we no longer truly hear it. Or maybe we've been talked at for most of our lives about what the Bible says we should and shouldn't do rather than being inspired and challenged and energized by who it says we are!

If we can get in the habit of renewing our minds about whose we are—which we will talk about more later—something truly does begin to change in us! Those who are alive in Christ are led by the Spirit, and those led by the Spirit "set their minds on the things of the Spirit." A mind set on the Spirit "is life and peace."[6] Out from that life and peace comes a rest that propels us, not just to do what is right, but to love God with all our hearts, minds, souls, and strength and to love others as ourselves.[7]

If you have ever looked down on yourself, ashamed and unworthy because you don't wake up each day loving God with all your heart, mind, soul, and strength, these feelings are not from God. God does not shame His own. The Enemy of your soul, however, will do anything he can to make you give up on living the Christian life. He knows that if he can shame you about some aspect of your faith, you'll likely keep your distance from God. Satan knows about the superpower of surrender that we explored in chapter 3 and how it propels us to live out from God. When we give up our own wants, desires, and need to control, God's Spirit can freely work in us and through us. And guess what? This is also where a love from God's own Spirit will rise up in us and fill our hearts with a genuine desire to be near Him!

Here's the thing: God in His grace and love has prepared for us a place of rich blessing if we will step into His commands. In fact, did you know that God's commandments— His precepts, statutes, rules, and instruction—are one in the same with His covenant love over us? In the Old Testament, His commandments cannot be separated from His covenant promise and ultimately His rescue, as He declared, "I will take you to be my people, and I will be your God."[8] Again, Satan is always on the prowl and would love nothing more than for you and me to see God's way as binding and restrictive, but, Beloved, God's guardrails have always been for our growth and His precepts for our protection. His commandments "are two-way words whose first direction is grace. They are words that create and sustain relationship."[9] They were never meant to be a burden; they were ever intended to be a blessing.[10]

This doesn't mean that obedience guarantees a life without trouble—again, Jesus already assured us that we would have trouble in this life. But one thing I know to be true: His way is the beginning (and the secret) of a life propelled out from a heart of rest. Choosing to follow the command to "put on the new self" *therefore* leads us to a deeper understanding that we are God's chosen ones, holy and dearly loved. And *therefore* we are able to put on compassion, kindness, humility, gentleness, and patience.

Living in God's commanded blessings doesn't mean that we won't mess up and grow weary. It just means that we will know exactly who to run to when we do! Jesus faithfully meets us on the other side of all our hustling and striving and bids us to come home in repentance and therefore *rest*.

It's precious to me to look back on those phone calls with Eric and realize that God was forming a timely message of rest in his heart too. A decade later, Eric and Kristin would pen these words in their book, *The First Breakfast:*

> In the gaze of Jesus, the way He sees is not determined by how we show up, or our reputation, or what we do *for* Him. He sees us through the filter of His own Covenant with us, and that makes everything look different. . . .

There is no need to strive, to try to measure up, or in the same way, hide or self-protect. He is initiating and extending a Covenant with us, that is based on who He is and what He has already done. And because of that, freedom and rest are available to our souls today.

His Covenant with us is greater than our commitment to Him.[11]

Beloved, the already of our story is that God's covenant love for us determines our identity and even our influence in this world. I don't know about you, but I find contentment and rest knowing that my commitment to God will always flow effortlessly as I choose to live from His promise over me. It reveals a clear distinction, a chasm really, between how we show up for Him and how He has already shown up for us!

True rest is in our surrendering to the already of our story and, by the Spirit of God, living it as only we can!

FOR REFLECTION OR DISCUSSION

1. Think of a recent challenging conversation or encounter with someone in your life. What would it have looked like in that situation to love that person out of your own strength? What would it have looked like to love that person out of God's strength?

_____

_____

_____

_____

2. Review the list of signs of outer-ring living on pages 59–
   60. Which ones, if any, are you most likely to experience?
   Why do you think that is? What other signs of outer-ring
   living might you add to the list?

   _____

   _____

   _____

   _____

5

THOSE WHO
LOOK TO HIM

THERE I STOOD, HUFFING AND PUFFING IN MY CLOSET, standing over a pile on the floor of four or five outfits that were just *not* working. Even my clothes felt constricting and irritating. Overheated from drying my hair and already running late to a meeting, I pulled several different sweaters on and off.

All I could think about was how I felt pulled in a thousand different directions. A pair of bricklayer's overalls seemed the most appropriate outfit as I considered the many-tiered life I felt I was supposed to keep building. My to-do list felt monstrous, and on top of that, I had procrastinated in picking up some hard-to-find specialty items that our youngest daughter needed for her scheduled dance studio pictures that evening. So rather than embracing my day and my family—my closest community of the Beloved—from God's love, I braced myself for the day ahead.

Before I had even begun to juggle the day's events, I was

already anticipating the struggle and how I would most likely drop the ball on *everything*. My eyes were downcast, my joy was smothered by obligation, and my heart was proud. I had once again strapped on the lie "It's all up to me today, and if things go wrong, I might as well admit that I'm _____." And I filled in the blank, calling myself names in accordance with how the lie made me feel in that particular moment.

I know! I told you that we were going to start focusing on living from the inside out, and here we are. *Surprise!* Yes, you will have days that are glorious and amazing, but some days will look like this, even when you intentionally start out in the bullseye. In fact, I actually had started my day in Psalm 26, where verse 3 reads, "Your steadfast love is before my eyes, and I walk in your faithfulness." And wouldn't you know it, just as I emerged from God's Word, I was attacked and challenged on the very thing that I just read! I wonder if you can relate. Maybe even today you've called yourself names, discouraged by all the ways you feel yourself coming up short.

Eric, my brother/mentor, would call this moment an opportunity to lead myself well. I know that might sound like a self-help mantra, maybe even contrary to what I've been saying, because we're supposed to be Spirit led, right? *Right!* But leading ourselves well simply means posturing our hearts to be led by the Spirit of God even when we don't feel like it. It is deliberately choosing to live in the rest that God says is available to us today.

One of the greatest worship leaders of all time, King David, understood how to lead himself well. He wrote, "Why are you cast down, O my soul, and why are you in turmoil within me? Hope in God; for I shall again praise him, my salvation and my God."[1] David led his own soul in worship, even commanding his inner being, "Bless the LORD, O my soul, and all that is within me, bless his holy name!"[2] I find it interesting that David spoke to his soul, in particular, when leading himself to God. Understanding how we are made up of a spirit, soul, and body helps us tremendously in surrendering the whole of who we are to God.[3]

The Hebrew word for "soul" that David used is *nephesh,* which also means "living being" or "person."[4] The soul is made up of our mind, our emotions, and our free will. I love how our family friend Bill Gillham called these our thinker, our feeler, and our chooser. The soul comprises our longings and our passions, our appetites and affections, and David led these things in a deliberate direction, centering himself in God, his supernatural help.

Unlike David, I initially missed the opportunity to lead myself well that morning and instead let my circumstances boss me around. But as soon as I walked outside, it was as if spring had sprung overnight! The birds were chirping, bees were buzzing, and my mouth dropped open in awe of the bluebird sky above. It was as if all creation was bursting with song and praise, tweeting out the wonders of a much bigger story overhead! With the sun on my face, I took in a deep breath and let out a long sigh.

AN UNLIKELY BATTLEFIELD

As I crawled up into the seat of my SUV, I shut my eyes tight and imagined myself getting to run back home to the bullseye. I started the car and sat still for a moment at my steering wheel, realizing that I had a choice about how I would approach the remainder of this day. Yes, I felt overwhelmed, with my thinker already believing lies about myself and my day. My feeler just wanted to crawl into bed and watch Hallmark movies all day, and my chooser was on the verge of making the decision to be miserable, as well as to make everyone around me miserable.

Outright war was being waged right in my driveway in suburbia America. It might sound really harmless, this war on how we think, feel, and choose, but the Enemy behind it is extremely dangerous. In Scripture Satan is called a liar, a murderer, the deceiver, the accuser, and "the spirit that is now at work in the sons of disobedience."[5] He doesn't care what it takes; he just wants to keep us from living from the already of our story so he can keep us believing his fabricated story of who we are. He's all about getting our minds set on doing things our own way, or on what the Bible refers to as "the flesh," and I was certainly in the flesh that morning!

The Message offers this description in Romans 8 of those whose minds are set on the flesh: "Those who think they can do it on their own end up obsessed with measuring their own moral muscle but never get around to exercising it in real life."[6] Talk about exhausting! No wonder the Enemy fights to keep us here, on a road to nowhere!

I'm not suggesting a "devil made me do it" mentality. We certainly have a choice in the matter. But as we've just seen, our choices often begin with our thoughts and feelings. Hence, the vital importance of setting our minds on the things of the Spirit and putting on the new self, as we saw in the previous chapter.

In other words, leading our real-but-not-reliable emotions (as my friend Shannon would say) to our supernatural Help!

Romans 8 goes on to say, "Those who trust God's action in them find that God's Spirit is in them—living and breathing God! Obsession with self in these matters is a dead end; attention to God leads us out into the open, into a spacious, free life."[7]

A "spacious, free life"—or "life and peace," as other translations say[8]—is a life worth fighting for, wouldn't you agree? To fight effectively in this war, it is helpful to know what the Enemy can and cannot access. But even more important is knowing who we really are in Christ so we understand the weapons of our warfare![9]

Let's hear the good news first: you and I have been given a force field of protection in Christ, and we have the tools we need to resist temptation. It's my understanding that Satan cannot access our spirits because we have been born again of God's Spirit, and the Abba cry that was awakened in us at salvation testifies that we are indeed God's children.[10] The Spirit of God Himself is also our seal, meaning that this work that God has done in us and will keep doing in us is already sealed up until Christ comes.[11]

What work has God done, and what work is God still doing in us? When you and I trust Christ by faith, we can claim the promises of God! Such as the promise that we are given new hearts.[12] Even the ability, by His Spirit, to return to Him with our whole hearts.[13] As part of the new covenant—God's promise to us through Jesus—God has written His law on the tablets of our hearts and even our minds.[14] We were once dead in our sin and therefore hostile to God,[15] but in believing on Christ for the redemption of our sin, we became new creations, transformed entirely.[16] The old self—flawed, sinful, broken—was crucified with Christ and then raised to walk in the newness of life.[17] All this is reflected in the act of baptism, a symbol to the world that we are united with Christ both in His death *and* in His resurrection! This is our "exchanged life" put on display for all to see.

In addition to all that, did you know that we have ascended into the heavenly places *in* Him? I know that this sounds a bit out there. That's because it's a part of the mystery of belonging to God. In Christ, you and I experience two realities. We are present here in earthly bodies that have not yet been redeemed (but will be on that final day), while simultaneously, even though it's hard to imagine, Scripture says that we are seated in the heavenly realms with Christ.[18] This points to the life-changing truth that even here on the battlefield we get to share in Christ's victorious life and even His authority over the Enemy![19]

Everything I've just described is part of the finished work of Christ, protected entirely from the weapons of the Enemy. But while he cannot touch our identities, which are sealed up in the Spirit, he can tempt us to question them. And that's where he wages an unrelenting war.

On this battlefield, Ephesians 6 tells us to put on the full armor of God (because this is no small battle) so that we can take our stand against the devil's schemes. Though the Enemy cannot touch our spirits, sin can penetrate and even indwell our not-yet-redeemed bodies (if we allow it) by accessing our thinkers first, which gets our feelers in an uproar and forces our choosers to make some serious decisions.

Are you seeing the importance here of a mind set on the things of the Spirit? When our thinkers are set on things above, imagine how they protect and guard our feelers and in turn our choosers!

When it comes to this battle over our minds—this war on how we think—I've learned that Satan most often goes for the jugular with a direct lie against our identities. He contradicts what is already true of us. Think back on that commodity mentality we considered in chapter 4, the lie that says that we are more like a slave in God's family and keeps us trapped in outer-ring living. Another lie of the Enemy is an orphan mentality that says we are not even in the family at all. This is the exact opposite of the truth that we are loved daughters and sons of God! It opposes our true reality—that we are unconditionally loved and there's nothing we must do to maintain this love, nor can we do anything to change it. We simply believe in its saving, redeeming power over us.

You might know, or at least can imagine, the heavy cost of believing these lies, allowing them entrance into the sacred place of our identities and letting them tell us how to feel: "I am worthless. I am alone. I am too far gone to ever be restored."

Feelings have become the North Star of our contemporary culture. I believe this is because we have numbed out to the truth and succumbed to Satan's fabricated, counterfeit story of who we are. We agree with his lies, allowing them to distort our identities and settling into a twisted mindset: *If I feel this way, it must be who I am, and shouldn't I be true to myself?*

Dr. Bill Gillham, whom I mentioned before, observed that God's definition of a hypocrite is "pretending to be what you are not," while Satan's definition of a hypocrite is "acting contrary to how you feel."[20] I can almost hear the Enemy now, breathing out his lies as I started to lead myself back to the bullseye after my morning rush to the hustle that day. "You're such a hypocrite, Christy! You and your podcast and your book about trying to be the Beloved. You don't even know what you're talking about! You are a liar and a helpless mess!"

Choosing to take in a deep breath and breathing out the very breath of God from my own lungs, I crawled back underneath my Father's tender care right there in the car that morning. And you know what? This is not me being a hypocrite; this is me *being exactly who I am* as the Beloved of God! It is me being true, not to how I feel, but to who I am as a new creation.[21] This is where I *belong*.

Sighing softly, I lifted the eyes of my heart toward the Lord, humbling myself and asking Him to forgive me for agreeing again with the lie that it's all up to me. I confessed my sin in calling myself—His Beloved child—ugly names and in anticipating failure when He's already set me up to win. And as I've learned from my prayer-warrior friend—another lovely Lauren in my life—I verbally came out of agreement with the lies and the names that I called myself, literally taking those thoughts captive in that moment and making them obey Jesus, right there in the front seat of my car.[22]

I laid out before the Lord how I felt about my day. That I was worried about all that I was carrying and, of course, that all I wanted to do was veg out and watch movies with predictable and perfect endings! Then I chose, out loud with my words, to invite Him to come and live His life through me that day. My prayer sounded a little bit like this:

Jesus,

I come humbly before You and choose to take my place as Your Beloved. You bought me with Your very life, and I belong to You. I ask Your forgiveness now for calling myself ugly names and believing the lie that I'm alone and that it's all up to me to build a life for myself when You are the one building me! I come out of agreement with these lies. [I specifically name any other lies I'm believing about God, myself, or others.] I renounce them in the name of Jesus, and I ask You to speak to my heart, in this moment and all throughout this day, what is true! I give myself to You. I invite You to come and live Your life through me today as I accomplish the work You've laid before me.

In Jesus's name, amen.

Often after a prayer like this, I will sit and listen and give Him the floor of my heart to speak, as well as stay attentive to Him throughout the day. In John 10:27 Jesus says, "My sheep hear my voice, and I know them, and they follow me." My favorite part of this verse is where it says "and I know them." Often, you'll hear His voice as something that deeply resonates in your spirit because He *knows* you. It might be a scripture, a song, a picture, or a thought in your mind that gives life to you. It takes time to learn to hear from Him, just as it takes time in any relationship to truly learn how to listen and hear the other person's heart.

Right there in the car, my downcast emotions began to lift as I took Jesus up on the invitation He gave me that morning— through all the worshipful critters out here at our homestead that we call Keeper's Branch—to recenter my heart in who He is and to live out from His love again.

This doesn't mean that I didn't have to work hard that day and that I wasn't challenged in having to juggle so many important and even precious things. I realize that this whole farm-table-epiphany-with-Jesus and lying-facedown-on-the-carpet thing might sound like I'm suggesting we spend all our time lounging and leaving all the hard work to everyone else. I assure you that it's quite the opposite! Learning to live from who and whose we are teaches us *how* to work. There's really no way around hard work. The Scriptures even instruct us to work hard with perseverance.[23] It's just that part of learning to work hard is learning to work smart, and to work smart, we learn to live from the love of God that propels us, making more of our effort than is humanly possible.

A MUCH BIGGER STORY

I don't know if you have ever tried actual juggling, but it is ridiculously hard! As with most hard things, there are secrets to successful juggling—secrets that at first might seem silly and insignificant and even counterproductive but ultimately point us toward deep things of the heart. As crazy as it may sound, the secrets to juggling point us to the beautiful blessings of bullseye living, revealing how we are able to work from rest even as we work and do hard things.

Juggling Secret Number One

You cannot keep your eyes on what you are juggling. You must lift your eyes to see the arc.

That morning in my closet, my eyes were fixed on what I was trying to hold together rather than on the One who is holding *me* together. I love that God got my attention with that beautiful spring-blue sky as a way to lift my eyes to a much bigger and more beautiful story over my life! I think about how the Enemy tries to trap me in my smaller story and even make me feel shameful for the way I've acted so that I might resist drawing near to God.

But Psalm 34:5 promises us, "Those who look to him are radiant; their faces are never covered with shame."[24] Remember, Beloved, you can never go wrong in looking to the Lord! You will meet eyes with your creator, who loves you and knows His own strength and stands ready to show it on your behalf.

A. W. Tozer in *The Pursuit of God* spent an entire chapter on what he called "the gaze of the soul" and gave us several biblical references into the fact that *looking* (on God) and *believing* are synonymous terms. He concluded that "faith is the gaze of a soul upon a saving God."[25] He went on to say,

> Now, if faith is the gaze of the heart at God, and if this gaze is but the raising of the inward eyes to meet the all-seeing eyes of God, then it follows that it is one of the easiest things possible to do. It would be like God to make the most vital thing easy and place it within the range of possibility for the weakest and poorest of us.[26]

Just breathe that in for a minute. If you need to go and lie facedown on the carpet for a minute, you have permission!

You know whom this makes me hopeful for? You and me and *everyone.*

I so love that the instructions God considers most valuable and vital for us to walk with Him work in *every* economy and in *every* season of our lives.

Think about it: if life boils down to us hustling and building and achieving all our dreams, how is that inclusive of everyone in every season and in every economy? How does that include the Beloved today in parts of the world where they have to chug filthy water and fight to feed their children? Not to get off topic, but seriously, let's think beyond the American dream. We belong to a much bigger story! That story includes the multitude of the Beloved "from every nation, from all tribes and peoples and languages" that we will find ourselves shoulder to shoulder with around God's throne one day.[27]

I find it incredibly beautiful and encouraging that God made it so that anyone who puts her trust in Him now bears the highest calling in life: to be the Beloved child of God. And what's most vital to this calling—to keep looking to God—*anyone* can do.

Even in terms of a spiritual economy, think about the weak and poor in spirit among us. For those who are fighting through unimaginable brokenness and pain in their stories, who have had trouble rising to just do the basics today—God has made the most vital thing effortless. To lift the eyes of our weary souls to this God who never grows faint or weary. To lift our heads from our "brick making" and remember that we are the ones being built.[28] To stop pretending that we don't struggle and instead gaze up at the One who struggled on our behalf, once and for all.

Whether it's before my feet hit the floor in the morning

or even when I need to recenter my heart in the bullseye after a morning sprint to the outer ring, directing the eyes of my heart toward God propels me toward the life and peace that I'm longing for. Most often, when we willfully choose to direct our eyes toward God, our hearts will follow!

Juggling Secret Number Two

Success requires loose hands, positioned palms up.

This one pretty much goes against our nature, or at least it does mine. I know that in my own life, I instinctively go rigid and grasp things tighter when I feel the pressure of all I'm carrying. But I've learned that it's counterproductive to tense up and to try to choose my own way. In 1 Peter 5:5–6 we read, "'God opposes the proud but gives grace to the humble.' Humble yourselves, therefore, under the mighty hand of God so that at the proper time he may exalt you." I told you that my heart was proud that day in the closet, proud in the sense that I chose my road to nowhere in the outer ring rather than in God's grace paving the way for my day. And in choosing my way, I chose *sin*.

There, I went ahead and said it. If I don't, I'm not being true to my own gospel story. And herein lies that battle we've been talking about! We must continually go to war against sin, especially our own. The Bible says to believers in Christ that what is not done in faith is sin.[29] I know that feels overwhelming to hear, but again, I think these juggling secrets give us a visual reminder that the *most* vital thing is to look up today. In looking up, we humble ourselves underneath this God who loves us and is ready to extend grace! Looking up *first* places us in this posture of seeing God for who He truly is and the much grander story that He is writing over our lives. This causes us, almost without our realizing it, to release our clenched-fist grip on everything and go palms up in surrender.

It's interesting that both passages of Scripture that talk about resisting the devil actually quote from Proverbs 3:34 in saying "God opposes the proud but gives grace to the humble."[30] In humility, we lift our eyes toward God, and I can't help but believe that this helps us position our hands open—not only to trust Him with everything we're holding but also to receive from Him all that He has for us! Hebrews 11:6 says, "Without faith it is impossible to please him, for whoever would draw near to God must *believe* that he exists and that he *rewards* those who seek him."

Juggling Secret Number Three

It's actually not about catching but about throwing with freedom.

Contrary to what we might think, juggling is not at all about grabbing hold of the things we've released; it's about finding a rhythm and throwing with freedom. After urging us to humble ourselves before God, 1 Peter 5:7 goes on to say, "Casting all your anxieties on him, because he cares for you." The word *casting* here is the Greek word *epiriptō,* which literally means "to throw upon."[31] We can throw our cares on Jesus. First of all, because He said we could, and second, because He cares for us!

This is what I did that day in my car when I laid out, with a sigh, how I was feeling to the Lord. The Bible says that even our sighing is not hidden from God.[32] This is how attentive He is and how much He cares for us. You know the power of a sigh, especially for us women. It can straight *clear* a room if we need it to! But what about that subtle, little sigh in the hidden places at the end of a really hard day? The almost silent sigh that you think no one else notices or cares about. When you wonder whether your day's work has meant anything at all and it's hard to even articulate what seems to be weighing on you. Beloved, He sees you and your smallest sigh, and He cares for you!

If He hears our sighs, don't you think He's attentive to every word we say? To cast our cares on the Lord, we actually need to open our mouths, like I did that morning in the car, and tell Him how we're feeling. Something powerful happens in our out-loud confession to the Lord, both of our sin and of our trust that He is sufficient for all our needs!

In the beginning of learning how to live loved, I desperately needed this kind of access to God and even a heart language for connecting with Him. I needed a way to communicate with Him that was sustainable and real and rolled naturally off my tongue. He knew this, and He surprised me with just how real I could be and how real He would become to me. When I don't know where to start in the morning, I go to Psalms. I love that God gave us one hundred fifty poems and songs featuring the highest of highs and the lowest of lows—a beautiful collision of humanity with what's heavenly—as a way of leading our souls to look to God today and be led by His Spirit.

I know that my husband appreciates this aspect of my walk with the Lord because it means he's not always having to be the place where I put things! When we've been publicly or privately put down, you and I need a place to put it all down at Jesus's feet. It might be that we've been publicly or privately praised and we feel our heads swelling a bit with pride. We can take it to Jesus and lay it at His feet. We can bring Him the fruit and the fear, the compliments and the criticism.

As we look to God—eyes up, palms up, casting our cares on Him—we see Him in a new light, we see ourselves in a new light, and imagine how it frees us to see *others* in a new light! It changes us from the inside out to *live* inside out. Sure, our to-do list isn't going to get done on its own, but our day is reordered around first things first as we're propelled to work from rest. Notice what happens when you start as the Beloved—look to God, humble your heart before Him with palms up, cast your cares on Him—then you choose to build up the people around you before you choose to build anything else.

Again, I'm so grateful that God comes and fights for our hearts!

As I looked to God to recenter my heart, what changed about me that day? I carried a marked sense of His presence with me, and I experienced a shift in the way that I saw myself, my family, and everyone that I encountered. One of the first things I did after I talked to Jesus that morning was call my husband to apologize. Because I had chosen a hissy fit over helpful communication, he had no idea what was going on or how he could help me. Come to find out, he had some margin to run some of the errands on my list and he was happy to help. I just needed to go palms up and *ask!*

With Nathan sharing the load and me realizing that a couple things on my to-do list could wait, I was able to get everything done with time to spare. Sometimes choosing a heart of rest involves being honest with ourselves and honest about our agendas, recognizing that we actually can't and don't have to do it all. When we invite Jesus to live His life through us, we find ourselves on His grace-paved path, where His way of doing life is easy and His burden is light.[33]

I was ever grateful for that lightened load when Annie Rose came bopping down the stairs to ask if I would put the finishing touches on her hair and makeup for her dance photo that evening. *I was all hers.* My decision to put all my weight on my gospel story changed the outcome of Annie Rose's day too. She was able to be mothered in those moments by a Beloved daughter rather than a stressed-out bricklayer.

As I held her breathtaking little face in my hands, I memorized her countenance as a way of saying thanks to the Lord for helping me see her and love her well that day. I got the privilege of twisting her beautiful, thick brown hair into a bun before Nathan and I drove her to get her dance picture made. (We both went because she's our youngest and the last one to take dance and therefore the last one to take dance pictures in a pretty dress!)

As we fully trust in God, redirecting the eyes of our hearts toward Him, quite often the things we're juggling fall into rhythm as they were meant to, freeing our hands to receive all that God has for us today. The most treasured gift that He has for us—besides Himself—is the people He has entrusted to us.

Chances are, God even now is moving people into the general vicinity of *you*. He knows that when you live out from His love, no one can better love them than you. The most beautiful and effective way to change lives around you is to let God change you. The best way that you can love others is to let God love you.

FOR REFLECTION OR DISCUSSION

1. When was the last time you felt overwhelmed by the day ahead and discouraged about the ways you seemed to be coming up short? What are some practical steps you could take to recenter yourself the next time you realize you are racing in the outer ring?

   _____

   _____

   _____

   _____

2. Consider your to-do list for the next twenty-four hours. What might shift in your heart and in your approach to the list if you first looked to God, humbled your heart before Him with palms up, and gave your cares over to Him?

   _____

   _____

   _____

   _____

PART TWO

The Community of the Beloved

LIVING FROM THE BULLSEYE OF GOD'S love changes the way we view God and others. We emerge each day as "those personally experiencing God's agape love"[1] and move into the community of people that He has called us to love.

We were never meant to approach one another from our own small love but to live out from the everlasting love of God as we engage those around us. We were also never meant to sprint to the outer ring on our own but instead to receive others—as we ourselves have been received—and to be the kingdom of God *together*. Romans 15:5–7 says,

> May the God of endurance and encouragement grant you to live in such harmony with one another, in accord with Christ Jesus, that together you may with one voice glorify the God and Fa-

ther of our Lord Jesus Christ. Therefore welcome one another as Christ has welcomed you, for the glory of God.

When we live out from this God who endures and encourages, He also grants, or supplies, us the ability to live in such a way that our lives sing in unity, to bring glory to God. As we love one another, out from the love of God, we extend His love, demonstrating to the barren world around us what it looks like to abide in God's love.[2]

6

THERE'S NO
BRASS RING

SINGING HAS SERVED AS MY CHILDREN'S KRYPTONITE over the years, my secret weapon to weaken the defenses of stubborn toddlers determined to resist nap time. Even now, when I'm running errands with those toddlers-turned-teenagers, if the afternoon sun starts shining into the car and Mama starts singing softly, chances are they'll drift off to la-la land in no time.

As ironic as it sounds, singing over my kids didn't come naturally to me at first. When you have a toddler and a newborn, you're going on about four years of being tired if you include the pregnancy sleepies. As we know, being tired can make you a bit cranky, and being cranky can make you just plain selfish sometimes. As I mentioned before, in the early years of parenting, I often rushed through meaningful moments like the bedtime routine. After all, I had emails to check, books to read, commentaries to study, journaling to catch up on. I wanted to get to my *real* life stuff—you know, all the things that were going to make me a better me!

Don't get me wrong. I'm a big fan of a bedtime routine that gets the kids down at a decent hour and makes room for some me time. It's just that in all my rushing to get to the stuff of life that I thought truly mattered, the makings of real life were right there beneath my nose! As God continued to reorient my heart toward home, He faithfully kept placing in front of me what He truly values and treasures in this life: His *people.*

God has lovingly and strategically blessed you and me, as the Beloved, with community, including our own families. He knows that one of our greatest needs is to belong—to be seen and known, to be gathered up and treasured. In living from the bullseye, from the inside out, we allow ourselves to first be seen by this God who made us and loves us. By design, this healthy union with God then spills over into our communion with others. The more we trust and treasure God, the more He entrusts to us what He treasures most. If you'll notice, even in those concentric circles that He's spoken to me through so often, it's people before productivity. Community leads us into the supernatural capacity that God has reserved for His Beloved.

As we learn to prize the people that God places in our lives, even before our own dreams, wants, and longings, we walk into a beautiful inheritance that far exceeds anything that we could have achieved on our own in the outer ring of our capacity. Something supernaturally glorious happens when we invite others into our experience of belonging and being treasured by God. The more we continually relinquish to God how we want our lives to unfold and trust Him with what He's put inside us, the more He entrusts us to care about what He's unfolding in others.

I first noticed this pattern through the simple act of singing over my kids at night. I will say, parenthood in general forces you to look beyond yourself and care for the needs of others, sometimes whether you like it or not. Singing to your children, on the other hand, is a kind of nurturing that engages both your heart and theirs, even if singing is not your thing. It slows your pace and directs your gaze. It's vulnerable, I know, but it captivates and communicates the heart like nothing else can.

Far from the spotlight of singing in front of crowds, the nursery rocking chair became my stage each night as I cuddled my tiny audience. This became our nightly rhythm. The kids not only would count on it, but they also began to have favorite songs and would often call out requests. When Noah was just a toddler, many nights he'd lay his little head on his pillow and say, "Sing Minna Minna Morning." This was his adorable way of asking me to sing "Love Him in the Morning," an old worship song that I had learned as a kid and now joyfully sang over my own kids.[1]

Our middle child, Elliana, wasn't one to call out requests at night. She always seemed quietly content to snuggle close and listen to whatever I came up with in the moment. It's funny, though—knowing her now, she probably had her all-request-hour list secretly stashed underneath her crib mattress and was just too shy to ask.

Our youngest, Annie Rose, on the other hand, would shoot for the stars every night! One evening I laid her down in her crib, her nightlight casting just enough glow to see her big blue eyes staring up at me as she sucked her fingers. This was her signature look back then, as her left index finger and middle finger were hardly ever not side by side in her mouth. She'd suck those two fingers and then pull them out when she wanted to say something. The best part was that when she'd pull them out of her mouth, she'd hold them together out to the side, like she was cradling a Marlboro. Not on purpose, of course. She was just a toddler. One particular night, she was a *chatty* toddler. It looked like she was taking a little smoke break in her crib as she held her fingers out to the side to say, "Sing a song." After I asked her to use her manners and say "please," I prayerfully and gently began to sing a worship song that her daddy and I had written around that time:

> A mighty fortress is our God
> A sacred refuge is Your Name[2]

I gazed at her intently, genuinely praying that those words would seep into her soul.

That was when she pulled those fingers out to the side again and said, "Can you sing 'all the single ladies'?"[3]

True story. Kids will keep you humble like nothing else will!

These moments of singing over my children, even the funny and unexpected moments, began to teach me the art of seeing them and treasuring them for who they are. I've heard it said that singing to God is the ultimate reconciliation of our hearts to His. Isn't that beautiful? I happen to believe that this actually works horizontally as well. I believe that singing over others is synonymous with seeing them and valuing them. You might have noticed that I keep saying "sing over." This is because I like to think of it as a declaration over others, to believe something to be true of them on their behalf.

Some nights I made it a point to sing directly *to* my children, as a way of showing them that I see them. Like the sacred moments, night after night, that I spent holding my beautiful, bashful Elliana, as this song began to stir in my heart for her:

Close your eyes, just be held
And hear me say how dearly you're loved,
When you rest, that is best
And you'll shine brighter when you wake up!
So, leave your hurry at the door,
You don't need it anymore;
The day is done and we can sing
while we watch it go.
Every day you're shining, dear,
Like the brightest chandelier,
But it's okay, just for a while
We can take it down to a glow.[4]

The most delightful thing about this song, to me—other than the fact that I sometimes still sing it to my now seventeen-year-old Elliana—is that it was fashioned from a heart that was learning how to rest. You can hear it when I sing it, and you can see it in every line of the lyrics. Those words bubbled up out of a heart that has learned how to be held by my heavenly Father, who always teaches His own that rest is best.

I can't tell you how many nights I've sung this to my own children, yet all the while, it's as if God was singing these very words over me. Yes, I often sang this song to Elliana to help her go to sleep. There's no denying that sleep is the kind of rest that our bodies need. Getting a nap is pretty wonderful too. Especially if you're a mama who still has toddlers, it's like going to a celestial ball! Yet, when I sing this song, even to this day, it's never lost on me that these words were birthed from a heart-and-soul kind of rest that comes only from that deep place of surrender and trust. I'm sure I sound like a broken record about now, but to authentically love others, we must first trust that we are loved. To hold others, we must allow ourselves to sink into the arms of our Father. To sing over others, we must first listen closely to the song being sung over us.

Be at ease. I'm not asking you to become Julie Andrews or suggesting that your mundane should look like a daily rendition of *The Sound of Music.* I love to think that our lives sing and that our song isn't limited to humming in the shower or belting out our favorite tune in the car with the windows rolled down or even worshipping through music at church. As a songwriter, I like to think that our song is our own personal proclamation to the world that we're here and we have breath in our lungs because of the love of this One who has put His very breath in us! Our lives sing about what we treasure. Our songs, whether sung or lived each day, rise up from God's song over us—His *life* in us. When we sing—when we live out from His life and we declare His life over others—this kind of God-song leaves a lasting impact and an enduring legacy.

GOD'S SONG OVER YOU

Did you know that God sings over you? I wonder if, like me, you find it hard to picture God as the kind of Father who sings over His own. I'll admit, I often project my poor parenting skills onto God and assume He's tired and cranky about having to take care of me 24/7! Sometimes I imagine Him with His hand on His hip, tapping His foot impatiently, wishing I'd just toe the line like I'm supposed to so He can get some much-needed peace and quiet. Maybe it's hard for you to envision yourself being soothed by your Father's song. Maybe your earthly father's arms were not a safe place to be. Maybe his song was dissonant and dark and caused a lasting pain in your heart. Or maybe he just never took the time to gather you up in his arms and let you know how much you're loved.

Wherever you are in this journey of living from God's love, you have a Father who sees you and sings over you. You are invited every day to be tucked underneath the mighty arm of the original Singer of life as He belts out His love over you. Zephaniah 3:17 says, "He will rejoice over you with gladness; he will quiet you by his love; he will exult over you with loud singing." That word *exult* there simply means "to delight or celebrate."

When I read this, I can't help but think of when my brother Eric sings "Happy Birthday" over his daughters. Eric excels at delighting in his girls. When it's time to sing to them, with candles on the cake, you can find him belting out his celebration over them! In fact, he'll even ham it up and won't give up until they are hysterically giggling. Beloved, did you know that God, too, makes a loud ruckus of rejoicing over His own? His Word is full of His song—His unfailing love over you—from beginning to end!

As I learned to tune my heart to God's song over me, trusting Him to fulfill my deepest longings, true contentment surprised me. I began to cherish His life in a new way and the lives of those that He has called me to treasure. I began to long for things that I had never before longed for or even thought to value. Awards and accolades from the outer ring shrank to the size of trinkets in my estimation as I began to supernaturally prize the people that God had placed in my care. Real and meaningful ministry was happening right there in my mundane, real relationship in my daily routine. I'd talk to the kids about the deep things of God, even though I knew that given their age, they didn't fully understand what I was saying. When my crankiness and impatience emerged and I blew it with them, you could find me on my knees—eye to eye with them—asking for their forgiveness. I'd pray out loud with them, even in the car while we were on the go, as a way to show them my deep need for God every day, every hour. I learned that I could be highly efficient in running my home while still being profoundly effective as I allowed my own Belovedness to spill out over my family.

LEADING WORSHIP WITH OUR LIVES

My friend Matt Redman, who is a worship leader, often says as he leads people in song that "seeing is singing." As we grow in our knowledge and experience of who God is—His attributes, His love over us, His faithfulness to us—we can't help but respond and sing with our mouths and our hearts and our lives. This is what worship is! It's our response to God that says that we see Him for the treasure He is and we can't help but sing! It's that beautiful reconciliation of our hearts with His that sings out, "God, You are enough—You are the life I've been longing for." We begin to teem with contentment in the inner places of our hearts, and we shake loose the old habit of trying to make a way for ourselves. We finally stop marching to the beat of our own puny little tunes, and we suddenly have space for the songs of others. In fact, the spill-over of our trust in God to make a way for us is that our *singing* also becomes our *seeing*. We look outward and we truly *see* the people that God has so strategically and lovingly placed in our care.

Since that day at the farm table, my home and my family have become a sacred place of rest and the birthplace of more songs than I could have ever imagined. Songs spilled out over the stove in the kitchen and in the backyard as my kids ran through the sprinkler. They happened at stoplights and in carpool lines inside my minivan that I called my sanctuary. Behind that wheel I'd lift up my voice in song as it seemed that the mundane became an endless cause of melody. This was truly where I learned to lead worship with my life.

One morning in the kitchen while we were getting break-fast ready, I spontaneously hugged Nathan tight in front of the kids. Noah was toddling around our feet, and Elliana was in her high chair. As we hugged, Noah ran over and wrapped his arms around our legs. We all stood there quietly, in a fam-ily embrace. We looked over at Elliana, and though she was just a baby, she grinned as if she knew that a family hug is a special thing. We've never talked about it out loud, but as the kids grew, we've reenacted this moment dozens of times over the years. When Elliana could walk, she'd run toward us, giggling with delight to get in on the embrace. The four of us would stand there quietly, as if we held the secret to life right there in that circle. And then there were five of us: Annie Rose was born, and it became one of her favorite things to experience the love of the family hug. Nowadays, when Nate and I hug in the kitchen, Annie Rose still comes running—even at twelve—along with our two dogs. No joke! Noah and Elliana usually just grin and give us a little nod of their heads from afar that says, "I do love you, but a family hug would be kind of awkward right about now."

One of those long-ago times, when the five of us were circled up tight, God spoke to me in the sweetest way as He whispered to my heart, *This is kind of like leading worship, isn't it?* I smiled as I realized what God was saying. When I spontaneously embraced Nathan in the kitchen that morning—the father of our home—the kids followed my lead. They wanted in on the embrace. And when I embrace my heavenly Father each and every day, this is an effortless and authentic way to truly lead people to embrace Him too. As I see Him, my life sings, and as I sing, my heart sees.

In these simple yet profoundly beautiful moments, God has schooled my heart on what is most valuable to and treasured by Him. As I learned the rhythm of resting in the bullseye, God began to little by little expand my capacity, showing me how to live out from His love. He began to bring to my mind faces and names of women. Some were local, some lived in other states, but most of them were gifted to write music, sing, or lead worship. I sensed God nudging my heart to reach out to these women whom I could specifically encourage in their fields and to gather them in my home. This helped me identify whom I could share my life with in that season, in addition to my family, and how I could help them live from rest. It was a place to start as I was learning how to live from the bullseye and then into the community that God had placed within my reach. You probably have people right within your reach in your trade or your lane of influence (even if they are online) who want to learn specifically from you.

I wasn't sure at first what I was supposed to do when we all got together, but this directive began to swell up in my heart: *Welcome others into your familiar with the Father.* I love that the Holy Spirit used words that I could understand. He knew that I know firsthand what it feels like to need a welcome. Part of it is because I've traveled all over God's green earth and I understand what it's like to be weary and to just want a warm embrace when you finally get to where you're going. A place to tie your hair up in a knot and go sock-footed or even put your pajamas on before dinner. The other part of it is that because I was once the weariest of the weary in trying to make a way for myself, a tune of compassion now played in my heart for other weary souls. This home that I'd get to welcome them into, a home where I once felt silenced and small, was now like a symphony hall where treasurable life was being beautifully and authentically conducted.

NO MORE GRASPING FOR TRINKETS

When this restful retreat finally came to be, all of us piled onto the couches in our family room with soft blankets and coffee cups. Many of these young worship leader women were young mothers or were about to be. I was a little further down the road than most of them in terms of motherhood and life, and I had been wrestling with some things that they were just beginning to encounter. There they were, bleary eyed, looking at me just as I had looked at Teri that day in the coffee shop. It was my turn to say, "You invite the glorious into the mundane." I wish I would have thought to say that in the moment. What I blurted out was much less eloquent: "There's no brass ring."

They all stared at me in silence and then looked around the room at one another, maybe because they had no idea what I was even talking about. Or maybe they were trying to decide whether they should be completely relieved or totally bummed. I broke the silence with "This side of heaven, we simply don't get to a place where we finally arrive." There's no perfect number of kids or just the right-sized house. There's no rung on the corporate ladder that will ever make you teem with lasting contentment. You'll never figure out the perfect balance of work and home. And even if you do somehow make a way for yourself, you'll always want more because there's no field to play on or stage to sing on that will ever fulfill the true longings of your heart.

Somewhere along the way, I picked up the phrase *brass ring* and knew that it was associated with striving for the ultimate success or finally arriving in life. But I had no idea where it originated. Not until I was writing this book did I finally look up where it came from. Back in the late 1800s, when carousel rides were in their heyday, often riders on the outer-most ring would feel cheated because only the inside ring of wooden horses seemed to teem with life as they bounced up and down. Because of this, the carousel operators would entice people to ride on the outermost ring by adding bonus experiences. One of them was a dispenser that you could reach out and grab a metal ring from as you spun past. It required a bit of skill to actually grab one of these rings, but if you were nimble, you'd get a trinket! Most of them were iron rings that could be thrown at a target, adding some extra fun to the ride. Every once in a while, though, a rider might get lucky enough to grab the brass ring. This was the grand prize because it got you another ticket to ride the carousel.[5]

This all sounds horrific to me. I'm one of those people who get sick on carousel rides. My kids have always known that either I need to *not* ride or I need to be the nerdy mom who sits toward the inside in something that looks like a sleigh, which is really just a glorified park bench for people who get motion sickness. I'm not kidding. I'm actually getting queasy just thinking about it now.

I also know what it feels like to become spiritually queasy, spinning around and around in the outer ring of my life while reaching for something that in the end doesn't really matter. To top it off, finally grabbing hold of what the world deems the grand prize gets me a ticket only to more spinning and striving and reaching. *No thanks!* Quite frankly, I think it's fitting that "finally arriving" in the world's economy is compared to an old carousel game, created to make sure that people don't get bored doing the same thing over and over.

THE TREASURE OF HIS SONG

That day as I huddled up with those beautiful songbirds in my family room, I marveled at how God had allowed me to struggle out ahead of them so I could echo back to them all that He was stirring in me. It wasn't easy to reveal my struggle. It was hard to open up my heart and admit that I didn't have it all together. But as I did, God seemed to give me courage to do it even more fully.

Only God could create a place of rest for our souls where the weak look strong and the vulnerable look valiant. Where we no longer have a desire to grasp for trinkets over and over in the outer rings of our lives. We want nothing less than to live in the treasure—the lasting legacy—of God's life song in us and through us. To let it resound as a welcome to everyone we meet.

One of the things I treasure most now in the reclaimed outer rings of my life is getting to lead women in worship. It's not lost on me what women, in particular, carry on a regular basis. Whether married or single, with or without children, women have a unique relational and emotional capacity to steward, manage, and lead their families and communities in a beautifully powerful way. So imagine how incredible it is when these multitalented, multitasking songbirds get shoulder to shoulder with each other in a room and start looking up toward God and singing. It's stunning! For this reason, I consider it one of the greatest joys of my life to get to stand before women—each with an incredible capacity to hold a lot of things together—and lead them to lift the eyes of their hearts and sing to the One who is holding them together.

It's not a stretch for me at all to picture you in this crowd of worshippers, where you get to enter the presence of your Father and lay down all your titles and responsibilities and just come as a loved child of God. To be filled with remembrance that your qualification to carry all that you carry and to lead what and whom you are leading and to love whom you love does not depend on you but comes from being His Beloved. Your life sings out from His song!

Lately when I've stood in some of these sacred moments to lead women in worship, the Lord has nudged my heart to sing over them instead. Sometimes even a lullaby. Maybe it's because He knows that I need to quiet my own heart to hear His song of rest over me.

Maybe you need to hear it again too.

> Close your eyes, just be held
> And hear me say how dearly you're loved,
> When you rest, that is best
> And you'll shine brighter when you wake up!
> So, leave your hurry at the door,
> You don't need it anymore;
> The day is done and we can sing
> while we watch it go.

Every day you're shining, dear,
Like the brightest chandelier,
But it's okay, just for a while
We can take it down to a glow.[6]

FOR REFLECTION OR DISCUSSION

1. Consider what it means to live out from God's song over us and to declare His life over others. Whom do you believe God has brought into your life today for you to see and sing over?

_____

_____

_____

_____

2. In what area of your life are you most likely to think, *One day I'll arrive. One day I'll feel fulfilled in this area?*

_____

_____

_____

_____

3. How does the image of God singing a song of rest over you resonate with your current circumstances?

_____

_____

_____

_____

7

COMPLETE MY JOY

A FEW YEARS AFTER MY FARM-TABLE EPIPHANY, I STOOD in our front yard and watched a handful of movers load that battered wooden table onto a moving truck, along with everything else from our beloved Tennessee home. I found myself in the middle of a lesson in how living from the bullseye creates space for adventure.

As I had learned to slow my pace and to lay down the habit of controlling our calendar, I watched our family become more available to God. As I looked to Him, relied on Him, and enjoyed Him, I found that my own plans looked measly compared to His intriguing mystery.

Now we were moving to Atlanta to help plant a church, which would start in a basement with just a handful of friends. Pulling out of the driveway that afternoon and trying to hold myself together in front of the kids proved to be one of the more bittersweet moments of my life. Noah was a rising second grader, Elliana was headed to kindergarten, and Annie Rose was one year to the day. I didn't want them to sense any distress around us moving. But leaving the first home we had purchased—where we had cared for our children as babies, where I had learned what soul rest truly looks like—was *gut wrenching*.

Nathan stayed one more night in the old house to make sure that everything was loaded, while my parents followed me to our new home in Georgia to help me navigate things from that side. Since we wouldn't have any furniture upon our arrival, we planned to have a campout in our den that night. We brought sleeping bags and pillows and an ice chest for food. The kids were in heaven to get to pretend we were roughing it in the woods for a night! However, a cloud of gloom settled over our glamping site when a summer storm hit our suburb and knocked out the power in the entire neighborhood. Suddenly, this big new adventure of a home felt like a scary, unknown place where none of us wanted to be. In the heat of Atlanta, it doesn't take long to start feeling a power outage in the middle of the summer. The kids squirmed in their sleeping bags, in the stuffy air, whining for the one person who wasn't there, of course—*Daddy*.

As I lay in the pitch dark, I couldn't even see my hand in front of my face. It felt like a stark reminder of how I couldn't see what our future held in this strange new place. God had been faithful to light the path up until that point, even leading us to a home where the previous owner had etched Matthew 11:29 in stone next to the front door: "Take my yoke upon you, and learn from me, for I am gentle and lowly in heart, and you will find rest for your souls." Yes, His goodness follows the Beloved all the days of our lives, but for some of us prone to outer-ring running, He sometimes etches it where we'll have to *see* it every day of our lives!

I knew that God had led us here. So why did everything feel so off and unfamiliar? I started letting my thinker and my feeler believe that it was even unfavorable. I started to doubt that we had done the right thing in leaving behind a ten-year season in Tennessee—a place we loved to no end—only to walk straight into what felt like a new level of obscurity.

Trusting God in the mystery sometimes includes asking Him for the grace, in the moment, to get past how things *don't* feel. Often we take that first step of trusting Him but then are broadsided with things not feeling how we thought they would. The Enemy of our souls loves to get in on this, of course! He specializes in making the Beloved feel unloved when life takes an unexpected turn. He'll even stir up lies in the middle of our murky mysteries, suggesting that trust in God mostly goes unrewarded, so why even bother? The truth is, when we trust God to make a way for us, often we're entrusted with what it feels like to not have "all the feels." Once again, herein lies the invitation to the real life we actually long for. As we push past our frazzled feelers and get our thinkers grounded in what's true of us, we remember that God can use every part of our stories, even the parts that feel dark and hazy or unfavorable, and turn them for our good.[1] Yes, trusting God is often like walking on a narrow, dimly lit path, but we move forward anyway because we never know what beauty awaits around the next bend.

As I lay there choosing to center my heart in the truth that

God knew right where we were and that He had us in His hands, the giant window in our den that looked over our backyard began to glow with a strange light. The storm had finally passed, and a breathtaking light show danced before our eyes. With all the house lights snuffed out, a cluster of what looked like a million fireflies in our tree-lined backyard lit up the entire room! We all felt completely dazzled at our own warm welcome to town.

THE BEAUTY OF UNMET EXPECTATIONS

I couldn't have fathomed it that night, but only months later, that den would become the site of another beautiful kind of glow. It would be filled quite often with the community of the Beloved.

Our little church plant was not so little anymore, and there was much work to be done. We were serving every Sunday alongside our friends, and God was moving in a powerful way. No doubt, it was exciting stuff! However, if you've participated in planting a church, you know that the work is never done. It's easy to experience burnout before you even recognize the warning signs. This mysterious adventure that I had looked forward to for so long—and yes, placed far too many expectations on—was not quite what I had imagined. As beautiful as the work was, I began to feel weary in it and even guilty that I didn't find more joy in serving. I couldn't figure out why I was so dissatisfied. Here I was again, trying to get past how things *didn't* feel.

Are you starting to see the pattern? God often speaks the

loudest right inside our disappointment and things not going as we hoped. We can get these social-media-sized ideas in our heads of what the perfect church, the perfect job, or the perfect family is supposed to look like. Then, just when we think we've arrived, we encounter another unexpected bend in the road or we recognize a longing in our hearts that somehow leaves us still looking for more.

It's these longings and even our dissatisfaction that we are invited to bring to God as we draw near to the familiar face of our Father. Did you know that you can ask the Lord how He wants to work in your life, especially in disappointment? One beautiful question that we can bring before Him every day is "God, what is it that You treasure for me?"

As I've listened for His answer to this question, I've had to lay down ideals and, let's face it, *idols*—things I've treasured above what God treasures for me. Things I've held on to just in case God didn't come through in the way I wanted Him to. This kind of surrender and confession is one of the things God desires most for us, as it's all about the refinement of our hearts. Not only has God lovingly restored us to Himself through His precious Son, Jesus, but He is also making us more like Jesus every day. Malachi 3:3 promises that His refiner's fire will not destroy us but purify us like gold. As we return our hearts to Him, He returns to us and keeps refining us as His "treasured possession."[2]

I don't know why I'm surprised to realize, every time I'm challenged to reexamine my heart, that God's refinement and leading in our lives is all about who He is making us to *be* rather than a list of things that we're supposed to *do* for Him. I've come to understand that our service to God is not what

He treasures most for us. That's a tough lesson for this church-going Jesus girl to get inside my noggin! What God treasures most always satisfies deeply, and service is not what satisfies the soul.

Approaching God and His people from service alone is like attaching a trailer to the front bumper of your SUV. Your only destination is frustration! What truly satisfies us and births in us the supernatural capacity to serve is resting in our citizenship in God's kingdom—taking our rightful place of sacred belonging to the family of God. We see here again that the order always matters, and the right order brings with it an overflow.

Our Belovedness, as you know by now, is forever centered in whose we are. Owning our citizenship, the truth of our sonship or our daughtership, is the God-created order for awakening a true servant's heart within us. If we try to maintain or keep earning our sonship or our daughtership through service, we are in danger of harming our ability to endure in the kingdom of God. We'll snuff out in no time, exhausted from the effort! We'll also likely get into a vicious cycle of service that is rooted in what we can get from God and others. This, too, will end in burnout, even sometimes fallout in community. This is that heart-barren, outside-in way of living where we try to conjure up the capacity to serve God and others in the mistaken belief that it will bring us that sense of belonging we long for.

Jesus modeled for us what it means to live in sonship as the Father's Beloved child. Hebrews 3:6 tells us that He served God's house "as a son." That same passage declares, "We are his house, if indeed we hold fast our confidence and our boasting in our hope." What a beautiful picture of our kinship with Jesus! It affirms yet again that He's building *us*. God is building for Himself a family, and we're His daughters and sons who get to live from a soul rest, a secure identity that sets us apart from all those hustling to prove their worth.

WALKING ARM IN ARM

I should have known that God's answer to me in that season would be to keep treasuring Him and what He treasures—to keep inviting others into my familiar with my Father, purposefully pursuing community before capacity. And that's what I did. I used every birthday in our family and every holiday—and even made up my own holidays—as an excuse to huddle up with this little flock we had grown to love.

Home and family and gathering around the table have always been God's dream for how the church would express His love. I believe God showed me that the community of the Beloved sits in the middle ring of those concentric circles, just outside the bullseye, for a reason. It's like that old children's book says, "We can't go over it. We can't go under it. . . . We've got to go through it!"[3]

As we return to God every day and live out from His love, it ultimately propels us into the beauty of creating community, even a sense of family, with others. To get even more specific, I've found that you can't live abundantly in your God-given capacity as the Beloved without first living in true community with others. I've watched up close how capacity— our ability to do even the good work of the kingdom—

quickly fizzles when community is not cherished. I believe that we are supposed to not only treasure community but also walk arm in arm together into kingdom things, to colabor alongside the family of God.

We enjoyed gathering families and single friends regularly in our home, but the group that God put on my heart to gather most often were the women worship leaders from every area of our church—from the mainstage vocalists to the young women who led worship for the toddler classes. These women gracing our home became a familiar and favorite routine. Most of them would drive from the city out to our place, where the crickets and frogs sing to you after supper. In they'd file, with fresh faces and topknots, filling every quiet corner of our home with the vivacious roar of women bright with Jesus. My own two daughters got to witness it all, feeling delighted by a couple dozen big sisters who, in turn, taught me how to mother beyond just my own children. As it turns out, singing over my kids was just the beginning of God's birthing a mother's heart in me.

It snuck up on me, this space in my heart that simply wasn't there before. All of a sudden, I longed for these precious women to know how dearly loved they were. I remember wishing I could somehow squeeze them tight enough that the awareness of their Belovedness would just stick. If I took their faces into my hands and spoke words of life down into their hearts often enough, maybe they would know that they don't have to work so hard to belong. This is when the Philippians 2 part of the vision Lauren had shared with me before my farm-table epiphany—this call to look into the interests of others—truly began to blossom in my heart.

If you mother or mentor, you already know that most of the time our influence lies not so much in what we say but in who we are and how we model to others who we are. Like that family hug, I would need to just keep running to the Father and embracing Him in front of these women. Because our church exploded fast, they were used to seeing me sing every Sunday on a big bright and shiny stage. It was tempting to hold on to that glittery facade. It would have certainly been easier in some ways. But deep down, I knew that wasn't what they needed. They didn't need me to pretend or present myself as one more unattainable standard. They get an overload of that every day. What they needed was a place to not have to pretend. A place where they could say out loud, "I'm struggling." Even more than a place to say, "I'm not okay," they needed a safe space to take that "not okayness" to Jesus over and over again. To get them to open up, I'd have to open up first. To get them to even bleed a little about what was really going on in their lives, I'd have to hemorrhage about what was going on in mine!

When all else failed, what always worked was simply sharing a meal together. I'd pull in card tables and end tables and toss tablecloths over them—whatever it took to get these women to sit across from one another, communing by bread and candlelight. (Okay, it was probably more like chips and salsa by candlelight. Either one is a win!) Sometimes we just went potluck, and my kitchen island turned into an assembly line of whatever tickled the fancy of those wonderfully creative and contagious women. Everything they brought to the table delighted me because I delighted in them!

After a few months of our journeying together, one of the

young women said to me, "Thank you for being real about where you are with Jesus because we can see that what He's doing in you is not just for you. It's for us too." Her words that night affirmed for me what it looks like to raise others up. *Our own refinement is the language of our discipleship.* We don't need fancy and persuasive words; we're just meant to tell others what God is bringing us through. His work in us is what we have to share. As I said earlier, I wholeheartedly believe that God is bringing people into the general vicinity of *you* because of what He's brought you through and what He's put in you to share.

And here's the thing: you don't have to fill your home with dozens of people. You can simply walk with one person at a time. What can you share? Whatever you have! If you're anything like me, you may worry sometimes that what you have to offer others won't be relevant for what they're going through. I assure you, if you have a story with God, then what you have to share is relevant.

Jesus modeled this so perfectly. He embodied what it looks like to live in community with the Father and how that authentically spills over into our community with others. Jesus retreated often to get alone with His Father. He spoke of how everything He did flowed out from His Father. Even as He served, healed, and ministered, He made known the posture of His heart: "The Son can do nothing by himself; he can do only what he sees his Father doing, because whatever the Father does the Son also does."[4] Jesus's service to God spilled over from His sonship, from His deep understanding of what it looks like to lead by choosing to follow His Father.

When Jesus discipled others, He pulled a few close and even invited them into His ministry. Jesus made surprising choices in carrying out His Father's plan. He didn't choose scholars or even students of the Scriptures. He found the most ordinary people He could find and invited them to walk with Him. He didn't look down on them, nor did He wait until they fully got it. Jesus strategically invited them into kingdom things with Him because He was raising them up to *be* the kingdom. He didn't lord over them with rules and demands; He gave them an up-close and personal view of His ministry, which as we know would include His being crushed. He hemorrhaged to the point of death on our behalf.

Knowing that at the right time He'd exit the stage, Jesus encouraged His disciples with the promise that they would do even greater works than He when the gift of the Holy Spirit came.[5] Jesus told us that the Holy Spirit is our Helper and that He would teach us all things and bring to our remembrance all that Jesus said.[6] Walking in step with the Holy Spirit positions us to align our lives with the Father's heart and to mirror Jesus's posture of serving from His sonship. The Scriptures mention the fellowship of the Spirit, which I believe is a special familial joy that's reserved for this precious family that God is raising up. When we live out from God's love and intentionally begin to grow others up in His love, this joy rises up in us, along with the abundant fruit that a life in step with the Spirit brings.

THE INSIDE-OUT PATH OF RELEVANCE

Molley is one of our dear family friends. We first met when she was a college student. We needed a backup nanny one night, and she was able to fill in last minute. We loved her right away and had her back multiple times to watch the kids. She and I both laugh now about how, at first, our pantry alone was a ministry to Molley. For a college student far from home, a home-cooked meal was like a slice of heaven.

As I got to know Molley better, I recognized in her the heart of a worship leader even before she did. Though she was timid at first, even afraid to sing in public, she had a deep compassion for people. Some moments in those early years, she'd sit on our couch with tears streaming down her face, telling me how much she longed to write music that would help people find freedom in God. Little did she know, God would answer that prayer by fully unlocking a heart of freedom in her first. Then He put His work on display for others to see.

Over the next fifteen years, I walked with Molley through some of the most vulnerable moments of her life, watching her surrender as much of her heart to Jesus as anyone I've ever seen. I watched that surrender birth freedom and refine her heart into gold. I watched it strengthen her song, even opening her actual singing range wider than before. When you live from your Belovedness, it's like a master class for living in your fullest God-given capacity. In Molley's case, it was like the best singing lessons she could have ever received.

I will never forget when I first got to see Molley lead worship publicly. It was one of the first nights since our church's beginning that I wasn't leading onstage. The Lord had been teaching me to make room for others, letting me know that sometimes I'd need to move over or even exit the stage to help raise others up. This is a refining work all on its own. Sometimes we think that to stay relevant in this world, we've got to stake our claims, hold our positions, and be the best in our fields. When you're no longer the new kid on the block, you may feel the pressure to prove that you still have what it takes. Fear of becoming irrelevant fuels an urge to keep striving to be at the top. I've come to realize that the very thing that you think will keep you relevant may be the very thing that derails your influence.

The word *relevant* simply means "closely connected to the matter at hand." The generation coming up behind us—they are the matter at hand. And they need us. They need us to *see* them and cheer them on. They need us to move over and share the stage, whatever that looks like in our different fields. They need to hear what we love about them and even what we learn from them. This is what it looks like to stay closely connected to the matter at hand, to be there for those who want to do what you do. Invite them into what you do *with* you. This will make you relevant until the end of your days. What will make you irrelevant? Sprinting to the outer ring, staking your claim, and building your own fame. There's a shelf life to this kind of fame building, and I imagine it will leave you pretty lonely as well.

Watching from a dark corner of the auditorium as Molley led worship, I felt like I was watching a butterfly wriggle free from her chrysalis. As she began to sing, it was like heaven lowered into the room. She roared her freedom song and the room roared with her as she assigned every lyric and every note a direction to go. She didn't command the room with aggressive leading; she disarmed the room with powerful humility and authority. God put Molley's Belovedness on display that night, and it was astounding and unforgettable.

In fact, I had an immediate visceral reaction when Molley began to sing. As the tears fell, I began to audibly laugh and cry all at the same time. The music was loud enough that no one could hear me, so I just let it out! I realized that in all my days as a worship leader, even a traveling troubadour, no service or ministry opportunity had ever brought this kind of joy. As I searched for the words to articulate what was happening in my heart, the Spirit of God brought me these: *complete my joy.*

In that moment I understood, for the first time, what Paul was saying in Philippians 2:

> If there is any encouragement in Christ, any comfort from love, any participation in the Spirit, any affection and sympathy, *complete my joy* by being of the same mind, having the same love, being in full accord and of one mind. Do nothing from selfish ambition or conceit, but in humility count others more significant than yourselves. Let each of you look not only to his own interests, but also to the interests of others.[7]

Paul wasn't questioning *if* these things are happening in our midst as much as he was reminding us that an overflow of joy is the inevitable result of living out from God and His Spirit. If we are in Christ, if we're experiencing His love, if we're walking in step with His Spirit, then we have what it takes to live in true community with others.

Those words *complete my joy* in the original language mean to "fill to individual capacity."[8] Isn't it beautiful to think that in watching Molley lead that night, I was filled to individual capacity? The unexplainable joy came not from watching my own dreams be elevated but from watching someone else's be lifted up. It was a proud-mama kind of joy, one in which the victory is extra sweet because you walked so closely through the struggle to get to that moment.

Molley and I lead side by side quite often now, and it won't be long, I know, until I watch her become a spiritual mama too. She's well on her way.

I continue to be enthralled with the beauty of God's kingdom and His way. When we release our cause to Him, we're free to lift up the cause of others. In fact, I think one of the ways that God holds up our cause is by leading us to delight in holding up each other's cause!

In taking a little deeper look into the word *relevant,* I found that it comes from the Latin word *relevare,* which means "to raise, lift up."[9] (Seriously, you can't make this stuff up!) What a beautiful picture of what it looks like to stay relevant! And what a way to treasure the people that God has given us, to lift each other up and even help raise up the generation coming behind us.

Friend, if you belong to God—if that Abba cry has been awakened in you too—then you have what it takes to have a meaningful ministry in the lives of others. His desire is that you'd embrace your own identity as His Beloved child so that you might raise others up to do the same.

You might be thinking, *How will raising others up promote a heart of rest in me?* In approaching others from the bullseye of God's love, I believe that we supernaturally experience the order we see in Philippians 2. By living out from our own encouragement in Christ, out from the comfort of His love and the participation with the Spirit, in humility we will consider others more significant than ourselves. So already, we are free from striving and we are positioned to experience the promise of Proverbs 11:25: "Whoever refreshes others will be refreshed."[10]

When we make *others* the matter at hand—cherishing community before capacity—I believe this unlocks in us a soul-restoring joy and even an unexplainable contentment and rest as we treasure each other and *together* become the kingdom He's called us to be.

FOR REFLECTION OR DISCUSSION

1. How did Jesus's awareness of His Belovedness impact His approach to serving others?

   _____

   _____

   _____

   _____

2. Why would God use relationships with others to complete our joy? How do those relationships glorify Him?

(Hint: Review what we learned from Philippians 2 on pages 116–17.)

_____

_____

_____

_____

3. When has someone ministered to you out of who she was rather than what she did? Whom might God be calling you to pour into right now, and what steps could you take to make that happen?

_____

_____

_____

_____

8

AMARYLLIS PRAYERS

I NEED TO TELL YOU THAT GOD HEALED MY EARS. I'VE quietly pondered this in my heart for some time now, ever since the day that my specialist walked in waving my hearing test results and saying, "I rarely see this kind of recovery! You need to go home and have a party!" He was right; I probably should have shouted it from the rooftops as soon I got to the parking lot. It really was miraculous news! I texted my husband as soon as I got outside. Then I crawled into my car and sat at my steering wheel—the same steering wheel I had stared at five months earlier while I tried to make sense of the hearing loss diagnosis that had just been dropped on me.

The whole ordeal, from beginning to end, had been such a struggle in the secret that it seemed most fitting in the moment to celebrate in the secret too. It's peculiar, this time we're living in. How we feel the pressure to market our

moments—sometimes pitching and posting too spontaneously a sacred experience that might have been better served
and held in hidden places, at least for a time. This felt like
hallowed ground as I sat in the car and had my own little
party with Jesus. Only He knew the depths from which I had
cried out to Him in those days as well as the heights on which
He faithfully would set my feet again. He alone knew the
prayers I prayed and the songs I sang as I combated the lies
that seemed to swarm all around me. The Enemy of my soul
had whispered all kinds of falsehoods to get me feeling unloved, unseen, and uncertain about whether I should even ask
God for healing—whatever was going to be would be.

Often the only physical solace I could find was in the
bathtub with the faucet running. The rushing water drowned
out the roaring in my ears, and I could pretend for just a little
while that everything was back to normal again. I'd emerge
with pruny fingers and toes, having poured out my heart to
God and, yes, even asking Him continually for healing. All
kinds of songs stirred in those waters, melodies from my
childhood and even songs that I had written years before, not
realizing at the time that I was storing up praise for these
darker days.

Even though I didn't fully understand why God was allowing the physical trauma to my ears, I chose to see His
heart and I couldn't help but sing. One morning the song
that stirred in me was something that I had written seven
years earlier. "My Master" was inspired by Exodus 21, where
we read about Hebrew slaves choosing to stay with their mas-
ters even after they had been declared free to go. To show
their allegiance, they would allow their ear to be pierced with

an awl against the doorpost of the master's home and they would say out loud—the same words I sang that morning—"I love my Master; I will not go free."[1] I held the earlobe of the ear most damaged, as if to say, *You are Lord over my ears; You are Lord over me. I choose to rest in You.*

As horribly frightening as that season was, within it I enjoyed a sweetness with the Lord. My desperation afforded me a beautiful dependency upon Him. As odd as it sounds, I miss it. Am I forever grateful that He healed my ears? Absolutely! I want to live in the wholeness of the life He offers. But I have to say, I wouldn't want to have missed out on the healing or the struggle. Both spurred on a deeper trust in God and led to even more rest in that season than I even knew I needed.

HIDDEN PLACES

The saga surrounding my ears oddly aligned almost exactly with the winter season outside that year. It was as if I slipped into winter, body and soul. As I shared before, my hit-the-ground-running plans for the new year became frozen in time as I blanketed myself underneath my bedcovers, watching snow fall. I felt like a fragile little fruit tree being wrapped in protection against the freeze. Over the years I've learned that big, public moments don't necessarily yield the best fruit in our lives. The choicest fruit grows in the unseen.

Hiding underneath my covers has become a familiar practice over the years. At the risk of sounding completely weird, when I was first learning to live in the bullseye, I would practice remembering that I'm covered by God by pulling my bedcovers over my head! I'm talking about a spiritual covering, of course, but sometimes the comforter on my bed is a good visual reminder. God's covering of love isn't limited to when I'm struggling; I actually most need it when I'm flourishing, such as right after I launch a new album or speak from the heart to a group of people. In fact, the more public my cause, the more I find myself running to my bed and crawling all the way underneath the comforter so that I'm covered head to toe.

Many times, underneath those covers, I thank God for the responsibility of getting to lead people, while in the same breath I release to Him that very responsibility as well as the people I get to lead. It's tempting to crave a response from the people we're loving and leading. I've found that I love and lead best from a deep place of rest when I continually release them to God, even out loud. This points back to our discussion in chapter 5 about throwing all our cares on Jesus—the praise and the put-downs—verbally casting them on the Lord.

Under His covering, I deliberately remind myself that I'm not more loved when I do things for God, nor am I more loved or important when I receive public praise. I also lead myself well in remembering that my public life will never be as important and powerful as my private life. This posture cultivates in me a heart of rest as I value the unseen and how the heart prospers most in the secret, with God.

We begin to carry a quiet confidence as the Beloved when we learn to be *made* in this secret place, when we realize that all our accolades and approval, our very rewards in this life, are found in who God is. The wonder and mystery—that we've been restored to this God who loves us—become our greatest joy. We find that all our longings are met with the glorious treasure of Jesus.

The pressure to display our treasures publicly lifts as we develop our sense of being grounded securely in the hidden places with God. What I've experienced is that the more we practice finding our meaning and worth in who God is, the more He unlocks new opportunities in the outer rings of our lives. We marvel, aware that this growth happened not by might, not by power, but by His Spirit alone.[2] In fact, as God becomes the treasure of our lives, often He unfolds the dreams and plans that we once longed for. But in a precious shift of perspective, those dreams and plans pale in comparison to the beauty and fullness and satisfaction that our hearts have already found in Him.

King David, whose role required him to lead a public life, understood the secret place with God. In Psalm 27:5 he wrote, "He will hide me in his shelter in the day of trouble; he will conceal me under the cover of his tent." This word *shelter* here means "secret" and is the same word that David used in Psalm 139:15 when he wrote, "My frame was not hidden from you, when I was being made in secret."[3] I'll venture to say that this secret place is one and the same with the bullseye of God's love. A safe place to hide from the pressures of this life and even the backbiting lies of the Enemy. We have a shelter and a covering where we can hear the healing whispers of God. He *is* the secret place.

IN THE BLEAK MIDWINTER

I remember, spring rushed in early that year as I slowly, in the secret, began to realize that God was restoring my hearing. The daffodils were the first to the party as always, and then all the other little sprigs of life began to show their pretty little heads too. I felt hesitant, not quite ready for the bustle and busyness that spring would bring. For this reason, I was over-joyed when we got a late snow that March. Partly because if it's going to be below thirty-two degrees ever, I would prefer there to be snow every time! And also because the snow seemed to make time stand still a little bit longer. It wasn't that I wanted to stay in a heap on my bed, in the struggle. It was more that so much growth was happening underneath the surface. Spring was beckoning, but winter seemed to be saying, "Don't forget." My spirit testified to the good work of winter—all that had happened in the season of struggle—and my heart ached to linger in the quiet with God.

I have to believe that this is because of God's faithfulness in winters past. I can look back on several seasons that shook me to the core—but I can also testify to the manifold blos-soms and branches that each one produced.

I recall a frozen wasteland of a winter that hit my family when I was only sixteen years old. I've mentioned that my dad has been a pastor my whole life and alluded earlier to the fact that outer-ring living took its toll on him in the prime of his ministry. My parents would tell you that their marriage suffered the most, and if it hadn't been for some necessary deaths during that brutal frost—a death to striving and hustling to find soul worth in places other than God—they might not have survived. Yet what the Enemy meant for complete destruction, God used to enrich the soil of our family and grow new life. As I watched my dad surrender his heart anew to God and my mother resolve to fight for her family through prayer in the secret place, something beautiful bloomed. And as only God can do with a heart surrendered in the struggle, we watched Him not only restore our entire family but also gloriously strengthen our roots all at the same time.

I can't help but think of another winter of my soul, maybe the rawest and most ruthless I've ever known. It seemed as if all the seams of my life had come unstitched and were left gaping open, exposed to the cold for quite some time. Have you ever had one of those winters? "If you've been up all night and cried till you have no more tears left in you—you will know that there comes in the end a sort of quietness. You feel as if nothing was ever going to happen again."[4]

My husband would tell you that the quietness lasted more than a year's time and that my verbal word count each day diminished to the bare minimum that I needed to get by. Because I belong to God, I had many times before felt His pruning as I trusted that He knew what needed to be cut away from my heart and when. But this particular time, it seemed as if He let me see for myself what needed to be pruned and He waited until I was ready to ask Him to cut it away, testing the resilience of my faith like never before.

What was so brutal about this winter? It was the sting of disappointment—life simply didn't go as planned. I know that may not seem unusual, but this loss sent pain shooting down every stem and every root of my life.

I've learned a great deal from this particular season. One of the most important things is that we have to be willing to own our part in things not going as planned. Please hear me out. Sometimes really disappointing things just happen and we don't play a part in it, such as when we lose loved ones to death. I'm talking about when we place our expectations or hope in the wrong person, place, or thing, which only adds to the pain of our disappointment. We might be holding on to some people or things (like those idols I mentioned earlier) just in case God doesn't show up in the way we want Him to. Only by prying our fingers from these things can we position our hands to receive the true abundant life that God offers.

God makes it really clear in His Word, over and over, that trusting in humanity leads to parched places in our lives. But consider this contrast:

> Blessed is the man who trusts in the LORD,
>   whose trust *is* the LORD.
> He is like a tree planted by water,
>   that sends out its roots by the stream,
> and does not fear when heat comes,
>   for its leaves remain green,
> and is not anxious in the year of drought,
>   for it does not cease to bear fruit.[5]

As I read this, I can't help but see blooms and vines budding up from the bullseye of our resting place as God's Beloved. Our trust in God waters us, grows us, protects us, and prepares us to yield the choicest fruit. It teaches us what's best for our roots: enriching time spent with God and His Word.

We learn to choose those things over and over as we gloriously grow into who God has made us to be. This is the way to life, but we don't always choose it, do we?

AWAKEN TO LIFE

My brutal winter of the soul happened well after my farm-table epiphany, and it seems I should have been long past placing my trust in people, places, and things. Is it just me, or have you unexpectedly found yourself in a wintry place and realized you'd chosen to walk down a path you'd once left behind? We can be comforted, even in the pain and pruning, that God is always about us becoming who He has created us to be. Even the vines that bear fruit He still prunes that we might bear more fruit.[6]

I wonder if you can trace some of the buds and blossoms you now bear all the way back to one of these cold and bleak struggles? Can you sit grateful today for what was cut away so that those new branches of life could spring up in you? What might still need to be cut away even now so that you might bloom to your fullest? Or does it seem impossible to believe that any good work could ever happen in a winter of the soul? Are you tempted to stay frozen solid, fearful that the thaw of hope will bring only more pain?

These are prodding questions, I know. But these were the questions that God used to awaken my heart out of slumber, and He used the community of the Beloved to speak them. I know I'm not right there with you, walking through your seasons and your struggles, but God is. And He can use any-one and anything to speak into the dead places of your heart and call forth life!

We need the community of the Beloved now more than ever. Again, we live in a time when it's easy to develop a false sense of community, believing somehow we are connected when instead we are dangerously cut off from those we need the most. We scroll through the big, bright blossoms of ev-eryone's lives on a minute-by-minute basis and wonder why we feel so small and fragile, frozen with intimidation. If we're not careful, we'll confuse the smorgasbord of social media with our *actual* community table, where what we bring is valued as unique and beautiful and vital. And Beloved, more than ever, we need to remind each other of what those things are!

God used the community of the Beloved to awaken my heart again, right in the midst of my raw and ruthless win-ter. Just like my very own Charles Dickens's *A Christmas Carol,* three vibrant spirit beings spoke into dead places in me—past, present, and future—and God used them to bring about a breakthrough beyond anything I could have ever imagined.

Lamentations 3 had been my song of lament almost daily in that season. I find it interesting that this passage is titled "Great Is Your Faithfulness" in the ESV translation, but the verses say things like "My soul is bereft of peace; I have for-gotten what happiness is; so I say 'My endurance has per-ished; so has my hope from the LORD.'"[7] True, godly lament always circles back around to His unending faithfulness. Even when we've lost all hope, we can choose to say "The LORD is my portion . . . therefore I will hope in him."[8] That was the choice I was making in that difficult season, but it wasn't easy.

The first person God used to speak life into my fragile heart was actually someone I had never met before. I was asked to attend a small prayer gathering hosted by a local ministry in our small town in Georgia. A few of my close friends who were there with me knew about the winter I was walking through. This made it all the more real and powerful when an older gentleman I had never met began to speak to me about it in front of the entire room. It was almost impossible to stop the tears when he said, "Christy, as I was praying for you, I saw you in a place of turmoil, and I saw strength and endurance happening in the midst of the turmoil." These were his exact words. I actually have an audio recording of the prayers from that night.

He went on, "You've learned patience, and you've learned that faith is the things hoped for and the evidence of things not seen. In the strength comes a depth of character—just like in the wintertime the roots of a tree grow very deep when everything is kind of blighted on the top and everything shrinks in, there's no leaves, no anything—that's where depth goes."

I began to sob almost audibly when he read from Lamentations 3, "I called on your name, O LORD, from the depths of the pit; you heard my plea, 'Do not close your ear to my cry for help!' You came near when I called on you; you said, 'Do not fear!' You have taken up my cause, O Lord; you have redeemed my life."[9]

He said much more than this, but it will remain in the

secret place and in the hearts of those friends I shared it with. The most important thing is that I left that night with hope in my guts again. As that stranger quoted those verses that had been my companions in the dark, it was as if God Himself was saying, *Beloved, I see you, I hear you, and I do love you.* My strength was renewed in the thought that there was great purpose in what I was receiving during my age of winter. I realized that even if I emerged from it all with God alone covering the gaping holes of my life, that in itself was healing enough. But God had more in store. He always does.

A few weeks crept by, and just as I began to think that maybe this people-speaking-into-dead-places thing was just a fluke, I got a phone call. I stood on my porch in the blazing Georgia sun as the woman on the other end of the line said, "Christy, I know you don't know me, but my name is Jennie Allen and we have a mutual friend that helped me find you." She began to tell me how God had led her to call me. She shared everything that He had been stirring in her own world and how, as a result, a thing called IF:Gathering had come to be and she saw me somehow being a part of it.

And this is the part where her words—which were really God's words to me that day—acted like a defibrillator on my heart. She began to call out things in me that had been lying dormant for months, maybe even years. Things that only God and I knew had long been buried for various reasons. Some by way of self-preservation, some by way of piercing wounds.

She reminded me of the call that God has placed on my life as a worship leader, someone who leads people to see who God truly is so that their lives might *sing* of who He is.

She shared with me specifically how God had used my journey over the past few decades, particularly in song, to many times meet her where she was. She prodded a bit by asking, "What are you doing right now to raise up the next generation of women in worship?" I have to tell you, I was getting a bit defensive and even a little irritated at this woman who seemed to think that she knew everything about me!

Now that I know Jennie, she's actually one of my favorite people ever. The woman will try anything, even walking through walls. With my voice shaking, I said something like "I don't know, Jennie. I don't wake up in the morning declaring that I'm the leader of the next generation of women worshippers. I wake up and make sack lunches and drive my kids to school!"

This is when I realized that there's a rhythm to living in the bullseye, and mine was a bit off kilter. Inside-out living calls us to hide in the center of God's love and then emerge from that hiding, every day, into the rings beyond. We begin our day with looking to God and placing ourselves underneath His covering. We consecrate our heart to His and, confident in our unshakable identity as the Beloved, trust that He will hold up our cause. We move outward to see others before we see the work before us. This is where I had slacked off. In the pain of winter, I was so busy protecting my heart that I'd become stuck in the habit of hiding. Some places within me even seemed to have fallen asleep. God used Jennie that day to nudge me and say, *Beloved, wake up. It's time to take your place again in all that I have prepared for you, and I want you to help others wake up too.*

They say that the third time is a charm. In November of

that year, I received a meaningful birthday gift from my sister-in-law Kristin, a trusted soul in my life. She had walked closely with me during my spiritual winter, and God used her in a powerful way to help me see all that He had purposed in my pain. Her gift to me was a potted amaryllis bulb accompanied by a beautiful, life-changing letter, which read, in part:

> We have this common thread in our family—we're drawn to the rich symbolism we find in the beauty of God-created things, like trees, vines and blooms. The way that a tree takes root, the way that a branch is nourished from the vine, the way beautiful things need necessary tending to bring forth more beauty.
>
> We love the marking of seasons and how we can trust that God is working in ways we cannot see. We know that every season is named with purpose. A season of sowing brings forth a season of harvest, just as the harsh cold of winter brings a season of dying . . . a necessary bridge to new life. The winter is beautiful under its blanket of white but it is cold and harsh to the living thing determined to grow. Everyone knows that the season for blooming is in the warmth of spring. Its gentle breezes and warm sun send a message to a sleeping world that all things are becoming new.
>
> It would take great courage to bloom in the bitterness of winter.
>
> But there are the rare and beautiful treasures that choose to grow when the conditions are the darkest. In the bleakness of winter, the Amaryllis will spring up,

pushing through the soil, displaying the beauty it was created to share.

Sure, it would be easier to wait until the comfort of spring. But the Amaryllis bulb knows it cannot wait. It does not bloom because the conditions are perfect, in fact, the conditions are counter-intuitive to new life. The Amaryllis blooms in winter, even still. It will not look to the world around it and depend on it for nurturing or care. It will instead, obey the world within it and become exactly what it was created to be. To bear the image of the beauty inside itself, set there by a Creator, not bound by time or season.[10]

The letter went on to tell me that my family would be praying "amaryllis prayers" for me, asking that I, too, would have the courage to bloom in winter. I realized in that moment that I had allowed my frozen, fragile state to render me ineffective. To keep me hiding until warmer, brighter days unfolded. I was overwhelmed by the kindness of God and the kindness of His treasured people to help me remember that stunning beauty can rise from even the most devastating winters of our lives.

I waited with such anticipation for something, anything, to break through the soil of that ceramic pot. Finally, one day a tiny, green shoot pushed up. As I watched it grow taller and taller and gloriously bloom that Christmas, I found myself pondering Jesus more than ever. He certainly didn't arrive when conditions were perfect. In fact, He arrived in the midst of a silence and a winter that the world had never known—four hundred years of silence, without a word from God. "And when it seemed like we'd never see Spring, Heaven gave a King."[11] Yes, He arrived when the world least expected it, pushing through the hardness of "winter" on our behalf. His love broke through so that we, too, could have breakthrough.

Beloved, maybe you need to hear it too: *Come awake!*

It's time to take your place in all that God has prepared for you, and He wants you to lead others to awaken too! He has and always will be the life you long for. No matter how dark and bleak your current season may be, you, too, can bloom with the brilliance of summer—right in the middle of winter.

FOR REFLECTION OR DISCUSSION

1. Where do you feel safest these days? It could be a place, a time of day, a relationship, or even times of pulling the covers up over your head! Why do you think you feel safe there?

   _____

   _____

   _____

   _____

2. As we've discussed, "inside-out living calls us to hide in the center of God's love and then emerge from that hiding, every day, into the rings beyond" (page 132). Is there an area of your life in which you are hiding even though

God might be calling you to emerge? How can you tell the difference between hiding under God's covering and hiding to protect yourself?

_____

_____

_____

_____

3. Describe a time when something beautiful blossomed in your life, something that would not have bloomed without your first experiencing a winter season.

_____

_____

_____

_____

PART THREE

The Capacity of the Beloved

WALKING ARM AND ARM WITH OUR BELOVED community as we live and love out from God's love over us,[1] we emerge into the reclaimed outer rings of our lives with God-propelled purpose and intentionality. When we live from this God-created order, our restful hearts rise up and contend for kingdom things together. Rather than making our own pursuits the prize, we treasure what God treasures.

In Philippians 3, the apostle Paul gave us a stunning picture of what endurance looks like as we live in our fullest capacity. He urged us to rejoice in Christ, to continue to be found in Christ, and to earnestly pursue our maturing in Christ. To "press on toward the goal for the prize of the upward call of God in Christ Jesus."[2] To *press on* is to "chase, like a hunter pursuing a catch (prize),"[3] and the *goal* can be translated as "a mark (on which to fix the eye)" or "an archery target."[4]

Beloved, our daily aim to hit the bullseye—this longing to make it our own because Christ Jesus has made us *His* own[5]—points us to our eternal aim, which is the perfect presence of Jesus forever!

9

—

HEART LIKE
A HONEYCOMB

I'D BE LEAVING BEHIND A SIGNIFICANT PIECE OF MY heart and my story if I didn't tell you about one other desolate season of my soul. Not that I want to wallow in winter, but I'd love for us to remember together that it's often underneath the blighted surfaces of our lives that we receive the very life we need to flourish. Again, spring will always beckon us with all that's bright and beautiful and busy, but winter proposes a pause to reflect and rest.

I shared earlier how motherhood happened to be one of the ways that God specifically chose to reach into my heart and change me from the inside out. It's been one of the single-most stretching areas of my life, well beyond the expansion of my belly. This is mostly because my entrance into motherhood didn't come about the way that I'd dreamed and planned. Long before my farm-table epiphany, God was planting seeds in my life to teach me about the depths of sur-render in the secret place.

As much as I hate to admit it, I brought my tendency to rush to the outer ring into our plans to start a family. This is a nice way of saying that for a while, I obsessed over Nathan and my moving on to what I had determined was the next best stage of our lives. Because we toured for a living, I was determined to have everything line up just right on the cal-endar so that we could fit everything in—doing the work we love *and* starting a family.

Certainly, nothing is wrong with baby planning. It's just that *my* baby planning included striving, worrying, and grasp-ing for control. I was convinced that everything needed to unfold perfectly and precisely to stay on my schedule!

Again, nothing is wrong with dreaming and making plans. It's actually responsible, rewarding, and even restful to prepare for the future. It's just that now that I've lived a little more life, I partner my preparations with the deep conviction that "in their hearts humans plan their course, but the LORD estab-lishes their steps."[1] But as we anticipated our first child, that was a truth I'd not yet fully taken to heart.

A SACRED SORROW

I well remember squirming around in that cold, plastic chair next to the nurse's station as I waited for my obstetrician to come in. I appreciated that the nurses were staying upbeat, trying to keep my spirit light by telling me that everything I was experiencing was actually normal in early pregnancy.

Unfortunately, I had been here before, so I knew all the early signs of a miscarriage. I sat and watched all the happy mamas with their basketball bellies pass down the hallway, holding their ultrasound photos, and I wondered what it must be like to get that far in the journey.

Quietly praying for a miracle yet again, I let my eyes wander around the room looking for something that might trigger me to wake up from what I hoped was just a nightmare. My eyes landed instead on a tiny painted canvas with some dried pink roses tied to the front of it. It said, in messy handwriting, "Be still, and know that I am God."[2] I knew it was the truth, but it still stung as I let it roll around in my heart with all the other things I was pondering—things like *Really, God? Another miscarriage?*

The nurse came in to take me back and hook me up to all the necessary devices that connected my belly to the fuzzy black monitor in front of me. I lay there and looked with longing on our tiny lima bean of a baby and had to hear once more those dreaded words, "I'm so sorry. There's no heartbeat." I couldn't even cry in the moment; I felt so numb and distant. It was as if some sort of protective mechanism was cocooning my heart from absolute devastation. At this point, I was grieving the loss of another baby but also battling the fear that something was truly wrong with my body. To make matters worse, it was a lonely battle because we hadn't told very many people about this pregnancy. We had already lived through what it feels like to announce to your entire world that you're having a baby, only to have to repeat over and over for weeks and months that it's not going to happen after all.

Those first few weeks of grieving, I slept, body and soul.

Each time I'd awaken, I'd have to reconcile myself to the fact that this was my real life. At first, I alienated myself and my pain from Nathan, forgetting that these miscarriages were a great loss to him too. I found myself building up an emotional wall between us so that I didn't have to fully deal with the pain or know what it would be like to grieve together. I figured out that I could even use harmless things to further distance myself from reality, things like ice cream and TV shows and even house hunting on the internet. Maybe buying our first home would somehow mend my broken heart! Occasionally I'd open the calendar on my laptop and count the days until I could possibly become pregnant again. In these restless and raw moments, God in His grace began to reveal to me, slowly but surely, that none of the remedies that I was reaching for would ever fix my ache.

One morning God showed up in the form of a basket of breakfast muffins and a handwritten note from a friend. I've kept it all these years as a way of remembering how God's Word is a healing balm like no other. My friend had carefully written out verses from Romans 5 for me, saying that we can "rejoice in our sufferings, knowing that suffering *produces* endurance, and endurance *produces* character, and character *produces* hope, and hope does not put us to shame, because God's love has been *poured* into our hearts through the Holy Spirit who has been given to us."[3] I remember reading the note out loud and clinging to each word as if it were a lifeline out of my current despair. This promise, that my suffering could somehow cause hope to be born in me again, was suddenly *everything* because I needed hope more than anything.

I began to think about how Nathan and I were limping

along, simply coexisting in the house but not fully allowing ourselves to heal together on a heart level. The Lord let me see Nathan's sensitivity in waiting on me to move toward him. Yes, he was ready to embrace me whenever I needed his arms around me, but as far as processing my pain, I would need to make the first move. Marriage is meant to be a direct reflection of life with God. Just as I needed to open my mouth and talk to Nathan about the pain in my heart, I needed to use my words with God as a way of leading myself toward the healing that only He could offer.

As I slowly began to open my wounded heart to God, I was surprised to feel alive again. I remember lying in bed at night, as close as I could get to Nathan's side, and imagining myself laying out all my longings before God, remembering that He is still better than anything that I could desire on this earth.

Eventually, I pried my little fingers off the house-hunting and calendar-counting strategies of my outer-ring baby planning and handed it all over to God. In letting go, it was as if my heart grew open hands to receive all that God had for me. I was suddenly aware that there were sweet and even sacred things that only this kind of sorrow brings, and there was wisdom in letting them do their work in my heart.

The more fully I surrendered, the more often I was surprised by rest and even joy. Nathan and I began to have fun again as we laid down the stress of worrying about when a baby would come. The sound of music began to fill our home once more, and new songs were birthed. We even finished a song that had stirred during our first miscarriage. I had tucked the lyrics away in a journal because it had felt far too painful until that point to even get past the first line: "Glory Baby, you slipped away as fast as we could say 'baby.'" As you can imagine, it had stung my heart to even go there, and fear rose up in me anytime I tried. Fear that if I shared the song, everyone would know my pain and I would have to talk about it. And then, what if I remained barren? Could I keep singing it and *sharing* it?

Because I've learned more and more about walking in surrender since then, I can look back and see the choice that was clearly before me. I could choose to view the struggle in my life as an infliction, or I could choose to see it as an *invitation*. In choosing to see the invitation, my heart stretched to hold and value things that I had never seen value in before—even the grace to hold and share the sweetness and sacredness of sorrow.

Looking with fresh eyes at Romans 5 and its mention of God's love being poured into us by His Holy Spirit, I can't help but think of the word *capacity*. It certainly relates to what we can produce, but it has just as much to do with what we can receive, contain, and hold. Again, I think there's divine order here—what we can receive and store up in our hearts determines the quality and the quantity of what we can produce. And get this: the word *contentment* can actually be defined as "the satisfaction of reaching capacity."[4] I love to think that this helps us reconsider what we mean by concepts like finding contentment and living up to our capacity. Not only is it possible for us to experience fulfillment in this life, but we can also find it in the fullness of what God has for us to receive in every season, big or small, weighty or light. Again, this is God's making it so that the most essential things in life are accessible to everyone, even when we're at our weakest and poorest.

I hope that you can see how it might bring true rest to your heart to recognize that living up to your capacity isn't dependent on your own output, strength, or ability; it is simply about what you are able to receive as you live from the heart of God. Even your darkest days of waiting can become the season that produces the weightiest blessings and fruit of your life.

A HEART WRAPPED AROUND HIS

You may have expected more active progress from the first chapter in the capacity section of this book. But I meant it when I said that the hurry-up-and-wait and the things-didn't-go-as-planned seasons of my life have always brought more forward movement and growth than anything else has.

As we've lingered here in winter a bit longer, I wonder how God might be whispering to you? Maybe you needed the assurance that He can use every part of your pain—past, present, and future. Maybe you needed to remember to hope for *hope* again! Maybe you've felt God's arms open to you and you've taken Him up on His embrace, but now it's time to open up and talk to Him about your pain, your longings, your fears, your need for Him. This is the crowning glory of your gospel story, Beloved, that God has made a way for you to draw near to Him and bring your all. Every weight and every wait, every winter, every sting of pain in your heart—He can bear it. In fact, He already bore it for you.

I wonder, can you pinpoint what He might be longing for you to receive as you draw near to Him? After all, a heart that looks to Him is postured to receive from Him, no matter the season. John 1:16 reminds us of what we're looking toward when we choose to look to God: "*From* his *fullness* [my concordance says "even (super) abundance"!⁵] we have all received, grace upon grace." *Grace* here in the original language carries the idea that God is "always leaning toward" us.⁶

If I had to identify one thing that God seemed to lean forward and extend to me right in the middle of the pain of my miscarriages, it would be the gift of compassion. Holding the sorrow in my heart of losing two babies has helped me identify in a specific way with those who experience this kind of tremendous loss. Compassion is at the very core of authentic ministry. I deeply needed this measure of compassion that God poured into me in those days to grow in all that He had purposed for me moving forward. Even now, that same compassion swells in my heart for you. I truly care about you finding the life you long for in this God who dearly loves you.

That compassion helped Nathan and me press into the pain and finish the song "Glory Baby" as part of our healing and memorial to the two babies we had lost—but also as a way of helping others through their losses. I never thought I'd be singing a lullaby to a baby that heaven would hold on my behalf. As Nathan and I kept trusting God with our future, we found joy in sharing all that He was teaching us through the trusting. Singing about our miscarriages in front of people wasn't what we necessarily wanted to be doing in that season, nor would we have chosen it for ourselves. But with it came an undeniable sense of contentment and a supernatural supply of strength.

That contentment yielded a season of consolation and even joy, as I shared before. So much so that I hadn't even noticed that I was unusually tired. Once it dawned on me, I knew before I saw the results of a home pregnancy test that a baby had come with no planning, no striving, no obsessing. I was at *rest*.

I remember quietly rejoicing as I saw that positive sign appear. I looked in the bathroom mirror and saw my own face sheepishly smiling back at me, and I heard the Lord say to my heart, *Believe*.

I chose to carry the wonderful news in the secret, quietly pondering it alone in my heart for a few weeks, along with this challenge from the Lord to believe that it would really come to pass. I remember driving in my car one day with tears of joy streaming down my face while I spoke prayers layered with gratitude and surrender. "Lord, thank You for this baby. I believe that You are going to let me have this one to hold. But, Lord, I love You more than anything. You can have this baby, too, if that's what brings You the most glory." I knew deep in my heart that I'd need to surrender this baby to the Lord at some point, so why not from the very beginning?

I do realize that this is a feather-ruffling kind of prayer, one that calls us to surrender whatever nest we're sitting on. This prayer might sound as if I view God as some kind of glory hog—like He's a bullying dream snatcher determined to make sure that we all get the spoonful of suffering we deserve instead of the life we long for. This is not God's heart for us. He is the way, the truth, and the life, and His life offers us something of infinitely greater eternal value than anything this earthly life can bring.

Do I believe that God had it in His heart to take my babies from me to teach me a lesson? *No, not at all.* But I do believe that all my days were ordained and written before even one of them came to be.[7] Did He say that we would have trouble in this broken world? *Yes.* But did He urge us to take heart because He's already overcome it? *He did.*[8] Does He desire and deserve our whole hearts in this life—above every person, place, or thing? *He does.* But I've realized that He will not stand in our faces each day and demand it. He gives us the choice.

All the wrestling and waiting in my life has revealed only a much deeper longing being fulfilled in me. The wrestling has also wrought my heart to start wrapping around His—a work that He is still completing in me to this day. A work that sets my heart on Him as the treasure, where everything dearest to me feels safest when surrendered to Him.

One of the most loving things God has ever done for me and my children and my husband was to show me that they are not the answer to my ache inside. Neither was a new house or my dreams unfolding precisely as I'd always hoped. Jesus *is* and will always be the one true answer to my ache inside.

When we consistently reach for the right Remedy and the rest that He offers, we naturally, almost effortlessly, begin to offer Him to the world around us. As the English poet William Blake observed, we become what we behold.[9] As we emerge from beholding the heart of God, we offer His peace,

His compassion, and His life to the world by the power of His Spirit within us. This is where the "quiet time" that so many well-meaning leaders have urged me to have finally began to make sense to me. However, I'm not sure it's as much about *having* a quiet time as it is about *becoming* the quiet time. Yes, it is vital that we get alone with God and His Word, but rather than a daily, transactional exchange, we were made to experience life-changing transformation in His presence.

TO PRAISE HIM IN IT ALL

Part of my God-propelled capacity continues to include singing over people from a place of rest. I've been surprised that some of these songs have come in the form of lullabies! In fact, I now have an entire collection of them called *Be Held: Lullabies for the Beloved.* I've discovered that we *all* need lullabies, as we never outgrow the need to be sung over or to even sing of the Father's love over our own souls.

I've sung these lullabies as a herald of hope over new mamas who need to hear that they truly will reap a rich harvest if they are faithful to keep tilling the fertile ground of their children's lives and hearts. I've sung them over empty-nester mamas who need to hear some praise for jobs well done. I've sung them over those who are still longing to become mamas, praying that the melodies will meet them where they are and carry them to the soul-filling love of God.

I've sung them over our precious children through the years, including that firstborn, who was born from rest. And I've sung them over my own soul—yes, some of these songs were birthed because I needed a song to sing in the middle of the night. I wonder if you'd want to sing this one too.

> Still this hurried mind,
> Smooth this furrowed brow,
> Bring Your heaven's song
> To my mouth somehow.
> With the rising sun
> Until the night has come,
> I will bless Your name
> For all that You have done.
>
> And hear me say, "Yes and amen,"
> Tomorrow You'll be faithful again.
>
> And I'll praise You, God,
> For all You are and all I am,
> For You are my portion, forever—
> For all that was, for all that is now,
> And all that is to come.[10]

It's one thing to praise God for who He is—and that's what we were made to do—but it's another thing entirely to praise Him for who we are. This isn't to the praise of us but to the praise of Him who has been our very portion in this life. To praise God for "all I am," I have to be able to praise Him and even thank Him for what He has and has not given me. As we mature in Him, we learn to trust that even His no to us is our best yes in every season. This ultimately invites Him—the One who casts vision over us like we can't even fathom—to show up on our behalf and surprise us. To help us see that the life we truly long for can show up in the most unexpected places. To remind us that our songs, our very lives, can be a powerful proclamation declared out from some of the most unexpected and even painful places in our stories.

To praise Him for "all that was" requires us to praise Him for even the things we wish we could undo, the pieces of our stories that we wish we could pull from the puzzle and fit something else into the frame. As we know, we can't change anything about what *was,* but we can entrust it to the God who *is* all-knowing, forgiving, loving, and restoring.

We can praise Him for "all that is now," even the current struggle we are sitting in, and believe that it might be the very means to help us recover our rhythm of drawing near to the soul-healing Remedy, who is Jesus.

And for "all that is to come," we can store up praise—even now—for uncertain days. As we remember Jesus's reminder that He has already overcome the world, we can relinquish to God any fear of the future and take heart in advance for all the flourishing in winter that is to come. That phrase "take heart" in John 16:33 is the Greek word *tharseó,* and it means "to radiate warm confidence."[11] How beautiful is that? Bolstered and strengthened within, we *become* the quiet time from which we sing:

> So take all that I dream,
> Take all that I plan—
> You hold all my days
> There within Your hands;
> Some days I might run,

Some days I might crawl—
But, Jesus, find my heart
Is Yours through it all.

And no matter what may come,
Make my heart like a honeycomb,
Storing up the sweetest home for You, in me,
Until I love You more than anything.[12]

As a songwriter, I sometimes find myself surprised by a phrase that emerges from my lips as I'm singing. "Make my heart like a honeycomb" is a perfect example of a moment where it seems as if God drops a creative thought down into the melody I'm singing—one that spurs even more thought later on—and I'm taken aback once again by the depth and beauty of our Creator God.

When I first sang about a honeycombed heart, I simply thought of how God designed us to receive and even store up treasures of eternal value in this home He has made in our hearts. I was reminded of the matchless beauty of surrender and the ability to praise God—even from a place of sorrow— for what was and is and is to come. The artist in me even imagined the hearts of the Beloved dripping with the sweetness of treasuring Him above all things.

But sometime after singing that phrase had become quite familiar to me, I stumbled on an entirely new and inspiring facet of what a honeycombed heart might represent for us as the Beloved.

STABILITY AMID STRESS AND UNCERTAINTY

When we find ourselves in times of difficulty, we can be certain they are not for nothing. As we learn to pray and sing cavernous prayers inside places of uncertainty, our hearts begin to expand and even strengthen over time. Like a honeycomb, the heart (the essence of who we really are) features a masterful design, reinforced by rhythms and order. I can't help but see this beautiful infrastructure being built in us over time as we choose to receive what God has for us in each season. Rather than being weighed down by the heaviness of our circumstances, we have the choice to receive the buoyant *fullness* of who God is, the One who offers grace upon grace.

For centuries, scientists have marveled over the perfection and strength in tension of the glorious honeycomb. In 1638, Galileo noted the sturdiness of hollow solids found in nature—such as honeycombs—stating that their purpose was "greatly increasing strength without adding to weight; examples of these are seen in the bones of birds and in many kinds of reeds, which are light and highly resistant both to bending and breaking."[13] For years, engineers have used the hexagonal pattern found in honeycombs to create products with a high crush strength-to-weight ratio,[14] such as cardboard boxes and crash barriers. In other words, they use a honeycomb design to reinforce various structures so they can absorb impact without collapsing.

The same week that my lullaby album released (along with my heart-like-a-honeycomb song), the *New York Times* published a fascinating article titled "Electric Honeycombs Form When Nature Gets Out of Balance." I found out about it by text from my friend Lauren, the same friend who shared the concentric circles vision with me so many years ago. Her text included a link to the article with the words, "Have you seen this???" Based on her usage of three question marks, I clicked the link right away. As I started to read, the hair on the back of my neck stood up.

Apparently there's a thing called an electric honeycomb. To properly explain it would take a lot of scientific talk, but essentially it comes into play when electrically charged particles travel but encounter a puddle of oil that would interrupt the electrical current without the emerging formation of an electric honeycomb. Here's the part that really grabbed my attention:

> This visualization reveals fundamental principles about how electricity moves through fluids that engineers can use to develop technology for printing, heating or biomedicine. But it also reminds us that humans aren't the only ones seeking stability in an unstable world. Even tiny, unconscious objects need balance.[15]

The other part of Lauren's text said, "The honeycombed-heart, it's not *just* for storing up sweetness, it's stability in uncertainty!"

Of course! I thought to myself. The surrendered heart, postured to receive from God, becomes a heart of *strength!* Even a heart of stability in unstable times. I wonder if the core of our human longing is not so much a search for the perfectly balanced life but a desire for a deep sense of trust and certainty in something bigger than ourselves.

Does the idea of encountering "a puddle of oil" along the way sound all too familiar to you, as it does to me? I think we'd both agree that it's a frequent occurrence on the road of life. Yes, we will always encounter circumstances that slow us down or make life unexpectedly difficult and painful. But what we *do* with life's interruptions says everything about who and whose we are.

Beloved, living out from God, we begin to trust *His* strength and *His* stability in us to absorb the crashes of this life. We get to collapse down into His confidence that *He* has created within us the ability to bend with the impact and not break. The grace to "radiate warm confidence" that He's got us. The remembrance to take on the shape of who *He* is. A robust faith that can sing in the face of all that is to come. And a heart of rest—what a gift of calm and certainty to the uncertain, clamoring world around us!—that invites others to sing with hope, "'Yes and amen,' tomorrow You'll be faithful again."

FOR REFLECTION OR DISCUSSION

1. How does the reality of God being the only answer to your deepest ache highlight His love for you?

   _____

   _____

   _____

   _____

2. Describe the difference(s) between a transactional relationship with God and a transformational relationship with Him.

   _____

   _____

_____

_____

3. When have you experienced the reality that "the life we
   truly long for can show up in the most unexpected places"
   (page 151)?

_____

_____

_____

_____

10

—

EVERYTHING
IS MINE IN YOU

AS YOU MIGHT ALREADY SUSPECT, I'M A WIDE-EYED dreamer. My husband, Nathan, on the other hand, is an investigator. This means that I can vividly see things for what they could be, but he holds the important element of knowing what it takes to get there. He's one of the rare ones who have both the spark and the grind: the ability to have his imagination sparked day by day along with the ability to grind out an idea and finish strong.[1] For this reason, for the past twenty-five years, Nathan has lived through, facilitated, put together, produced, championed, restored, and finished strong many of my ideas and dreams, as well as the dreams of other artists and worship leaders.

Nathan is an artist in his own right, but he would tell you that what he loves most about making music is producing music for others. I've heard him explain that it's like lifting that artist or that worship leader onto his shoulders and giving him or her a megaphone to reach the world. He's that behind-the-scenes guy who sits unseen in small rooms and listens intuitively to artists and songwriters. He often has an ear for that last song that the songwriter almost didn't have the guts to submit for the album, the song that the artist probably believes in the most but doubts that anyone else will get. Nate's the guy who gets it and says, "That's your best song actually"—and then helps bring it to life like magic, as he did with songs like "Blessings" by Laura Story, "10,000 Reasons (Bless the Lord)" by Matt Redman, and many others.

I mentioned earlier how sweet I think it is that Nathan's name is set down in the middle of what I consider to be my life's passage of Scripture. I discovered this just a few years ago, after my sister-in-law Kristin texted to ask if I had ever looked up the Hebrew word for "give" in Psalm 37:4, as in "He will give you the desires of your heart." Kristin loves devouring Greek and Hebrew words, and knowing that this is an integral part of this passage for me, she was pumped to share the news!

Immediately curious, I stopped everything to look it up and found that the Hebrew word for "give" is *nathan*. As I shared before, it means "to give, put, set."[2] Only recently have I seen the full beauty of what I believe that God was showing me through Kristin's text that day. As I think about Nathan and me and our wirings—how we do work together at our best—it speaks volumes to me about the capacity of the Beloved.

When Nathan and I work on a project together, we both have to lean toward the other to get in a good flow. It can be tough at times because we're married. Sometimes our pride wants to send us running in the opposite direction from each other! But I've realized over time that in order for me to real-ize some of my dreams—whether that's restoring a good-for-nothing house that everybody else gave up on or creating a lullaby album from scratch—I have to move toward him and I have to be in a right relationship with him. I also have to swallow my pride and let him know what's going on inside me. This includes spilling my guts on songs and ideas and dreams. Sometimes he takes the route that makes the most sense to me, and other times I can't comprehend why he's choosing the route he's taking. Either way, I've learned that he deserves for me to be still for a minute (which he would tell you is hard for me) and *listen*.

I can't help but think of how this insight could build up all of us. If you insert the Hebrew word into Psalm 37:4, it can literally be read, "Delight yourself in the LORD, and he will *nathan* you the desires of your heart."

I assure you, Nathan is very human and has quirks and shortcomings like the rest of us. But doesn't it make you think that if God could so intricately wire a mere human to help others display their Belovedness in this way, how much more is God able to infinitely do this on our behalf?

When you live in your God-propelled capacity as the Beloved—swallowing your pride, laying out your longings before Him, leaning toward His supernatural spark and grind, and trusting Him to help you—you'll find Him there ready to live through, facilitate, put together, produce, restore, bring to life, and finish strong the things that He's put in you to do. Will He always go the easy route that makes sense?

Most likely not, but I do know that our God loves to lift up on His shoulders those who choose to trust Him and give us a megaphone to reach the world.

TRUSTING GOD TO LIVE THROUGH YOU

Living in our God-propelled capacity, we don't have to strive to make known what He's put in our hearts to share.

This is good news for those who tend to talk a mile a minute, who bring bright and bold color to everything they touch, and who have enough spark to set the world on fire. If this describes you, know that you don't have to try so hard. You can trust as you work that God is going to move the message He's given you *through* you. You don't have to shout it from the rooftops or assume that it's all up to you. You can rest on His shoulders and rely on His miraculous megaphone.

It's also good news for those who are introverts, who might have a significant spark or the gift of grinding out a grand idea, or who maybe have the spark *and* the grind but color their world with tones that are softer, calmer, and subtler. If this describes you, rest assured that as you emerge out from God's love, you can trust Him to live His perfect life *through* you, to make known to the world—authentically and in a way that's true to your unique design—what He's put in you.

I fall into this introverted camp. In fact, a love of being quiet is something Nathan and I always agree on. My friends who know me well are probably giggling right about now in agreement. I think it surprises people because I travel and sing and have a podcast, but trust me, you can do all those things and more yet still be a quiet person. Being quiet doesn't mean that I don't want to be with people. One of my favorite things in life is what my friend Shannon calls companionable silence. It's a sense of belonging with family and friends without the need to be "on" or to fill up the space. It's deep fellowship, even in the glorious quiet.

Sometimes, though, I'm afraid that I might be misunderstood in circles of people who don't know me well. I'm an internal processor, so often in big moments I don't feel the need to spew forth wisdom—I'm taking it all in to ponder later. Sometimes I have to step into a leading role, but you can bet that any wisdom I share in those times was gleaned from a quieter place than the one I'm standing in.

Many of my friends are extroverts, and quite a few are authors and speakers. I marvel at their ability to think on their feet, to captivate a room or even just the dinner table with the roar of their stories that spur on laughter and deep thought. I truly enjoy the fact that I get to sit back and be entranced by their exuberance. Sometimes, though, I'll hear the whisper of our soul-killing Enemy that says, "You don't have what it takes."

When I let that lie get under my skin, I start hashing out in my head all the ways that I need to change or pipe up or hustle a bit to keep pace. I'll mentally rehearse past failures and times I felt the rejection of others—*What if my quiet is getting in the way?*—and I'll assess all the ways that I need to amp up my game to avoid being left behind in terms of my life unfolding in the way I want it to.

I'm not dismissing the truth that we can grow in our confidence and boldness and endurance; I'm actually heralding it. In fact, that's what this book is all about! God's rest *propels* us as we live from His confidence, boldness, and endurance. To have longevity in this life (and I believe that's what we're all after), we must protect our ability to live from God. We do this by paying close attention when we feel the urge to assert ourselves to see results or to rely on our connection with mere humans to keep us on the map. I know, it's strikingly countercultural, but so was Jesus.

True rest in God is trusting Christ's life through us to make known what He's put in us!

Again, this is not our lying around all day basking in our Belovedness. We emerge *from* it and into all that God has called us to. Hearts at rest—whether we are rambunctious or restrained—communicate to the world around us that God can be trusted with our capacity and our causes. Our posture of rest declares that we believe that He is the author of everything of true value in our lives. I mean, *hello,* He is the greatest content creator ever, and He's the one who gave us these gifts, ideas, and talents.

So He can be trusted with all He's put in us!

TRUSTING GOD FOR EACH YES AND EACH NO

I described earlier how I had yessed myself into exhaustion in the early years of motherhood and ministry. I was not posturing myself to trust in God but was believing those unsettling "you don't have what it takes" whispers from the Enemy. This got me depending on my own efforts to keep my life going as planned. I don't know about you, but even now with the best of intentions, I can still get in trouble with a crowded calendar!

Hearts at rest have learned how to trust God to be our promoter, to guide our yeses and our nos. My brother/mentor, Eric, challenged me once to think about the fact that we initially have a gut reaction to most opportunities that come our way. It might not be the case across the board, but for the most part, when certain opportunities arise, we immediately sense in our spirits a life-giving sort of peace and even an excitement. On the flip side, some opportunities bring on an immediate sense of exhaustion and obligation. We might even feel the weight of dread, yet we can't imagine saying no to what seems to be a big opportunity! In our God-propelled capacity, we must learn to pay close attention to these initial thoughts and reactions.

As the Beloved, we have the Holy Spirit of God dwelling in us. He is our inner compass who can make even our yeses and noes crystal clear.[3] Sometimes we'll have to wrestle with decisions, and yes, we should actively seek wisdom from the Lord. But as we learn to walk according to the Spirit (a mind and heart set on Him every day) these initial reactions will become more readily apparent.

I wonder if, like me, you've said yes to plenty of opportunities that were already a no in your spirit. Those are usually the ones that, on paper, seemed to be a great dream move but ultimately cost more than you gained in terms of peace of mind, family time, or some other area you wish you had better protected. It seems that the things we do to feed a hunger within us somehow always come back to bite us.

As you stay connected to God's heart in the bullseye, it truly will help you make healthier decisions. If He's prepared things in advance for us to walk in, wouldn't we need to draw near to Him each day and ask Him what those things are? Meeting with God is where we find the capacity to step into our yeses and the courage to determine our nos.

Sometimes we need to trust Him with a yes when we're not sure we have the capacity for it but we do have a genuine peace that in our obedience He will make it possible. Sometimes we need to trust Him with a no, believing that in our obedience He will fill any lack that arises—financially, emotionally, spiritually. I'll tell you this much: you'll never go wrong saying yes or no if you're leading with faith and trust in God! It might not produce perfect results in the moment, but over time you'll see purposeful results that you will forever be grateful for.

TRUSTING GOD'S RHYTHM OF REST

The spiritual mama heart in me desperately wants you to see that you have everything you need in Christ and His life of rest is yours to embrace. Just like my own mama said to me as a child, "If you give your heart to Jesus, He will show you the way to go." This isn't just for salvation; this is for everyday moving forward. The only thing you need to strive for is the rest that God offers you *today*. Again, this is not a sit-around kind of rest; this is you in your fullest capacity trusting God to hold up your cause in this life.

The book of Hebrews says a lot about the rest that's available to the people of God, but it is also brimming with warnings—warnings that we must be faithful in giving one another as the community of the Beloved—to not be deceived by sin but to trust God "just as firmly as when we first believed."[4] Another warning in Hebrews says, "We must listen very carefully to the truth we have heard, or we may drift away from it."[5]

The most alarming thing about drifting is that it happens slowly. Rarely do we make a mad dash for the outer rings. Though it may feel abrupt when you realize you're caught up in a performance cycle, if you look back, you'll note that some kind of compromise led you to drift into barren mode. Maybe it started with the age-old temptation to peer into someone else's lane. Rather than looking to God, we begin to ever so slightly look to the left and to the right. It can be as simple and subtle as scrolling up and down through the feeds on our smartphones. Before we know it, something has shifted in our hearts. It can be ever so subtle, like switching your headset to dance to a different beat at a silent disco.

I don't know if you've ever been to one, but a silent disco is an actual thing. It's a dance party where everyone in the room wears a headset that plays one of two or three different channels of music. Everyone dances his guts out along to whatever music is playing on his headset. The funny thing is, if you take off your headphones, it just looks like an event space full of people going completely bananas—in complete silence—for no apparent reason. When you put your headphones back on, you can look around the room and see that you're dancing to the same song as whoever's headphones are lit up with the same color as yours. Throughout the night, you can switch channels and look around to find who your people are.

In much the same way, we might be dancing freely and effortlessly in the rhythm created by the Conductor Himself when a little bit of FOMO sets in. Everyone around us seems to be going bonkers over a rhythm we're not hearing, and we feel a twinge of fear that we might be missing out. Curious about the beat of the crowd's rhythm, we switch over and try theirs for a while.

Something in us senses that dancing too long to this beat may lead to burnout, so we switch back to the inside rhythm of rest when we need to feel like ourselves again. Before long, we're switching over to the outside rhythm again and staying for longer periods of time. After all, it must have its perks because everyone dancing to this rhythm seems to have it all—the shiny *everything,* all the right stuff and all the right moves. Even though we don't feel quite ourselves around these dancers, we tell ourselves, "You should just be happy to get to be in the same room, let alone dance to their beat." Besides, when you dance the way you were made to, everyone looks at you a little bit sideways, with a twinge of shaming in their eyes.

Over time, your defenses weaken and you pretty much stay in the outside rhythm 24/7. After all, the only way to survive this rave is to just keep going. You've noticed lately that your breathing has become labored, but you ignore it for now because you've got to keep up. Thankfully, the dance moves are so familiar now, you could do them in your sleep.

One day, you notice someone dancing to a rhythm you

haven't seen in a while. As you give him a quick sideways glance, something about his dance stirs a memory deep inside you. You remember how you used to dance to your heart's content to that restful rhythm, making up moves on the fly. It was good and you knew it, and it brought you joy. You didn't need anyone else to tell you it was good because you had your eyes on the Conductor and He was smiling. You recall how the Conductor delighted in the dances you created to His rhythm. Then it hits you: the joy was never really about the dancing, was it? It has always been about this Conductor and His heart over you. He's the reason you got up in the morning and felt like dancing. He was your deepest joy. This memory sends an ache across your heart. Oh, how you've missed the Conductor. Your heart breaks to be near Him again!

Everything in you longs to rest, but vivid fears arise when you contemplate switching back to the inside rhythm. Fears that you might let down a lot of people. After all, you've become one of the lead dancers in the outer rhythm. What will people think? Conversely, you might fear that if you leave the beat of the outer ring, you won't even be missed. You're well aware of the backup dancers ready with bells on to fill your void. Worst of all is the fear that if you leave the outer rhythm behind, either you'll never dance again or, even if you do, no one will care.

Have you been here before? I suspect all of us occasionally find ourselves living in the consequences of a subtle switch of perspective, when our eyes have shifted from looking to the God of super abundance to looking to the camouflaged barrenness of this world.

Our only hope in this life is to run back to Jesus, the conductor of the rhythm of rest. Here we are met with eyes of mercy. We aren't even expected to dance right away. Maybe we need a minute to sit and listen and let our hearts be stirred from rest. To hide before we emerge. And that's okay. God knows we will dance again, and when we do, it will be from this very rest, in the light and effortless way He always intended.

TRUSTING GOD'S PROMISES THAT ARE ALREADY YOURS

I remember the day I met my friend Ellie over a songwriting date. I smiled as I watched her walk up to the house juggling her guitar, a big bag over her shoulder, a water bottle, and a huge Bible tucked beneath her arm. I remember thinking, *I like this girl already.*

After we greeted each other and settled in, she pulled out her Bible and I pulled out mine—because this is how all good worship songs should start. She scooted her chair up so that we were almost knee to knee. Both of us began to share transparently what was going on in our lives and what scriptures had been burning in our hearts. Come to find out, we had each been walking through some unimaginably hard things with people we love.

The scripture on her heart was Romans 4, where we are reminded about Abraham's faith. "Against all hope, Abraham in hope believed and so became the father of many nations, just as it had been said to him."[6] I think it's worth noting that a weary-from-waiting and childless Abraham majorly jumped the gun on God's promise to him that his descendants would be too many to count, like the stars. In Genesis 16, we read about Abraham and Sarah's outer-ring hustle in taking matters into their own hands, not fathoming how God could possibly accomplish the vision. This would end up causing trouble for years to come. You see, even people with great faith still have great doubt and run to the outer ring at times. But God is a God of mercy. Even though Abraham and Sarah royally messed up some things, God was still faithful to all involved, and Abraham learned to keep choosing to trust in God.

Ellie and I considered those words in light of our current stories, contemplating what it would look like to stand and hope against hope even in the middle of the unimaginable. The passage that I was sitting in was equally challenging. It was 1 Corinthians 3, where Paul said,

> Let no one deceive himself. If anyone among you thinks that he is wise in this age, let him become a fool that he may become wise. For the wisdom of this world is folly with God. For it is written, "He catches the wise in their craftiness," and again, "The Lord knows the thoughts of the wise, that they are futile."[7]

The Message version here says, "The Master sees through the smoke screens of the know-it-alls."[8] Paul went on to say, "So let no one boast in men. *For all things are yours,* whether Paul or Apollos or Cephas or the world or life or death or the present or the future—all are yours, and you are Christ's, and Christ is God's."[9]

Everything is already ours? Ellie and I sat together wondering how in the world you declare this in such a busted-up world. How do you utter these words—that are the very Word of God—when it feels like your world is tearing apart? When you feel utterly alone and disillusioned and all that's left is to hope against hope?

We began to sing anyway, and you know what? There was a lot of angst in it, and that's okay. We held both sides of the tension of what it looks like to walk through the unimaginable while claiming for ourselves the hope that *everything* is *already ours* in Christ. I've since realized that to be able to say, "Everything is mine in You, Jesus," we have to be able to clearly define what *everything* is. It can't possibly be a person, place, or thing of this life. Everything is the promises of God—promises that we can stand on in every high and every low, even when we're weary of waiting.

The song we wrote together ended up being called just that: "Everything Is Mine in You." I had the joy of leading this song with my friend Jorge not long after it was written. He looked over at me during rehearsal and said, "Christy, I feel *invincible* when I sing this song!" That was the heart and the hope: that anything we long for can *already* be found in Jesus!

Friend, as you own your Belovedness, you're going to see the outer rings of your life be reclaimed by the purposes of God. Your capacity will become less and less about trying to unfold the life you've always wanted and much more about you inviting others to find their own hope of invincibility in Christ.

All throughout this book, we've pictured God almost leaning over the edge of His seat, looking for those who will look to Him. But did you know He's also on the lookout for those who will stand in the gap on behalf of those who are not yet looking to Him?

Ezekiel 22:30 says, "I sought for a man among them who should build up the wall and stand in the breach before me for the land, that I should not destroy it, but I found *none.*" I memorized that verse in junior high at church camp, on our youth pastor's tongue-in-cheek orders at breakfast that we couldn't eat dinner that night unless we could recite this verse in the supper line. I doubt he would have really deprived us of dinner, but my friend Courtney and I were determined not to miss out on the delicious cooking of our church cooks. Their homemade rolls remain the best I've ever had! So we made up hand motions to help us memorize Ezekiel 22:30, and I remember it to this day!

Of course now I understand the incredible weight of these words, and there's much more on the line than pot roast and potatoes. As the Beloved, from the heart of God, we are here to *re-present* Christ and contend for a lost and barren world that needs the loving arms of this Father we know and love.

But how can we invite people in if we're racing around the outer ring, upping our game in competition with one another? If this is where we are, what do we truly have to offer this world? In glaring contrast, envision how when we live from the bullseye—from the rest God offers us—we are able to extend to this world who He truly is. What a life worth longing for!

I'm reminded of a seminary graduation address given by John Piper, which I came across when I was delving into the "all is yours in Christ" declaration of 1 Corinthians 3. I had to let it wash over me before I declared a few lines of it, a few nights later, over those dear worship leader women that I gathered often in my den:

> When a sense of insecurity in your abilities, in your job, in your ministry, in your theology, tempts you to attach yourself to someone stronger, someone more competent, more esteemed, more gifted, more secure, don't do it. You don't need to do it, because all things are yours. . . .
>
> When the craving for secondhand significance and worth and power and authority tempt you to grasp for it vicariously by boasting in men, don't do it. You don't need to do it, because all things are yours. . . .
>
> How can this be? Because you are Christ's and Christ is God's.[10]

Beloved, you *already* have it all.

FOR REFLECTION OR DISCUSSION

1. Describe a time when you said yes to an opportunity that was already a no in your spirit. What happened?

   _____

   _____

   _____

   _____

2. What activity, relationship, or commitment in your life
   today might reflect your striving to prove yourself more
   than your desire to live out your unique identity in God?

   _____

   _____

   _____

   _____

11

——

THE POWER
OF SMALL

"WELCOME HOME."

Nathan and I sat, bleary eyed, on the bus we had just boarded in Tel Aviv along with a small group of friends and family. The bus would be our portal to rest after what felt like a never-ending day of travel. Our Jewish guide, Shai, knew everything we didn't about the land that we'd be exploring for the next twelve days. He also knew exactly what to say, even before we could understand what he was saying. His words *welcome home* just seemed to sit on the surface of my heart as the bus began to roll and I looked out the window, having to convince myself that I was really in Israel.

I spent the first full day and night in a jet-lagged daze as I tried to comprehend things like standing on the remains of King Herod's palace and looking out on what was left of his swimming pool. That same day, I held in my hand pottery that is known to be from the time of Abraham and even led our group in the song "Waiting Here for You" from the top of Mount Carmel. These were monumental days, getting to see with my eyes the things that I had only heard and read about my entire life!

The second night, we arrived in Tiberias, where we'd be staying for the next three nights, right on the Sea of Galilee. This was one of the sites that I'd been most eagerly anticipating, but it was dark by the time we pulled in. It was just as well because I was so tired from the day's adventure that I could barely keep my eyes open.

I crawled into bed that night, fully expecting to fall fast asleep from fatigue, only to lie there and have my mind come alive like a movie screen. How could I be lying in bed only yards away from where such momentous miracles had taken place? Soon, the ominous waves of the Sea of Galilee filled my imagination as they threatened to engulf the disciples in their boat. I could see Jesus curled up at the stern, fast asleep, while the others feared for their lives. As the disciples frantically woke Him from His nap, Jesus simply rebuked the wind and said to the waves—the very waves I could hear rolling in outside my hotel window—"Peace! Be still!"[1]

My mind moved to the scene of Matthew 14, when Jesus gave His disciples the fright of their lives. He had sent them on their way in the boat while He went up into the hills to pray alone. When He returned, He found them far from shore and struggling against a strong wind. This is when He walked out on the water to meet them where they were.

Thinking He was some sort of spirit out to haunt them, they screamed in terror as He approached!

This is just the way my mind works, but since Jesus was the God-man, He knew everything, even the fact that He was getting ready to scare the daylights out of His friends. Maybe it's just me, but I can't help but picture Jesus chuckling to Himself as He sauntered across the water toward their boat. He knew that these guys were small minded and even a bit superstitious, but oh, how He loved them something fierce.

This encounter is incredibly endearing to me. Let's be real. If Jesus wanted to help these guys only navigate the strong winds, He could have just stood on the shore and told the wind and waves to chill out. I think this was all about Him taking their relationship to the next level by revealing more of who He really was to His beloved brothers. I can't help but think that it was a bit playful of Him. He knew these guys through and through, like He knows me and you. He had no doubt that Peter would be the first one out of the boat, asking if he could walk on water too!

The Scriptures say that it was sometime before dawn when Jesus walked out on the sea for His little ghostly greeting. It also says that as soon as Jesus and Peter got back into the boat, the wind stopped and the disciples worshipped Him, saying, "You really are the Son of God!" This is just my imagination, but I love to think how they might have quieted down in the boat together as the sun made its glorious entrance over the eastern hills. And maybe for just a few minutes, after the quiet, you could hear their laughter echo across the water as they reenacted in hilarity—as any close brothers would—the depths of how good Jesus had just gotten them. Speaking of the sunrise, I had to get some sleep! My alarm was set for 5 a.m. so that I could see a Galilean sunrise over those eastern hills for myself.

But before my alarm could go off, a local and very reliable rooster awakened the entire hotel before dawn. Nathan and I scrambled around in the dark, and I threw on a sweatshirt as we headed for the door. Nathan thoughtfully gave me some space so that I'd be alone when I opened the double doors of the hotel that led out onto the grassy ledge of the waterfront.

And there it was in all its glory. *The Sea of Galilee.*

Honestly, I've traveled all over the world and I've never seen anything more beautiful in my entire life. You know by now that I'm a crier. But I have to say, the wave of emotion that came over me that morning I hadn't experienced in years. The only thing that could come close would be the day that Nathan and I pulled away from our wedding in the getaway car. It might sound strange, but we held each other and sobbed. Partly because it really was the most beautiful and sacred day, but also because we'd just passed this historic and massive mile marker of our lives! And then it was quiet, at last. We were husband and wife and finally just *together.*

Now here I was standing at another historic mile marker, walking onto the cinematic set of Jesus's life on earth! When I was growing up, the stories had felt larger than life. Sitting crisscross applesauce in front of the felt board on Sunday mornings, I bought in—heart and soul—to the marvelous adventures of this famous Miracle Worker.

Yet as I walked toward the water that morning, the warm

air outside falling on my skin like silk, I was surprised to realize that nothing was ominous or momentous about the sea
before me. In fact, I still can't get over it.

It was *so* small.

So small it moved me. I mean, I knew that it was a lake
and not really a sea, but this was smaller than the lake of my
childhood summers. You can see all the way to the other side.
It seemed as if you and I could get on paddleboards and reach
those eastern hills in no time. That's right, it was small enough
for you and me. When you're standing there, it doesn't take a
cinematic-sized stretch of your imagination to find yourself
in the story. This was no larger-than-life movie set. This was
a tiny corner of the world where Jesus lived a real life with
real friends that He adored, whom He invited into real ministry with and to broken people.

I felt invited, too, and my tears turned into the kind of
sobs where you get those little stuttered breaths as you try to
breathe and cry at the same time. Yes, the scenery was breathtaking. The calm, the colors, the clarity—it was paradise. But
what moved me most was the fact that it felt so intimate, so
real and untouched. I became captivated by the fact that I was
looking at the sunrise from the same vantage point that Jesus
would have seen it countless times. These were His stomping
grounds. The place I imagined He loved like His hometown.
And these were all the familiar sights, sounds, and smells that
would have greeted Him on a Galilean morning just like this.

"You were really here," I whispered. Oh, but wait, "You're
here *now*." This is when Shai's greeting to us on the bus that
first day penetrated my heart for the first time.

"Welcome home."

THE INSIDE-OUT, UPSIDE-DOWN KINGDOM

You and I, we've been conditioned to all things ginormous in our Western lives. We tend to shop in giant stores, drive giant cars, and live in giant homes. Seriously, compared to most of the world, even a small American apartment is like a mansion. Even as we scroll through social media, we thumb through our larger-than-life "community," buzzing about all the big events. You might even scroll through my posts and find the details of the next big thing in my own little world.

Even church has become gigantic for many of us, complete with cameras, lights, and room-filling fog. I don't think it's because we're going for a disco feel; it's just that our culture has become acclimated to pleasing aesthetics that help things feel not so real and raw. Not to worry, this isn't a soapbox speech. I'm simply observing that we have become accustomed to all things big, bright, and beautiful.

Is it okay to attend big, beautiful events? Of course. And we certainly should not neglect coming together with the people of God. These gatherings are meant to unite us in worship, unite us in purpose, and even help us remember that we're not alone in the longings we carry. However, we can sometimes walk away from these events and back into the real and raw of our seemingly small lives only to be met with feelings of disappointment and even insignificance. We wrestle to reconcile the fact that our greatest efforts, on our own, seem to produce what look and feel like minuscule results.

A heart at rest deeply understands the importance of valuing the seemingly small moments of life as potentially miraculous, eternity-sized events. When we begin to understand what God can do with the small and unseen corners of our lives, this lifts our expectations from the big bells-and-whistles moments.

I can't help but think of some of the house shows that Nathan and I have participated in over the past few years for my album releases. (This just means that we sometimes give concerts in living rooms!) One sacred night in Texas around the release of my lullaby record, my dear friend Whitney opened her home for us to share the new songs with some of her friends. About a hundred women packed into her living room that night, women who are Whitney's Beloved community. During Christmastime, I'll get a few texts per week from Whitney that include pictures of amaryllis blooms sitting on the windowsills of many of these women's homes—bulbs that Whitney hand delivered to them as a way to mark God's faithfulness in their stories.

That night, I experienced the precious gift of knowing what it feels like to sing into *faces* rather than just *places.* I got to direct the truth of those lyrics into tearful eyes, right there in front of me, as I watched God use His truth, set to melody, to cradle the hearts of His daughters. A group of women attending that night literally carried, in and out, one of their dearest friends, a woman whose body was being utterly destroyed by cancer. She might not have had the strength in that season to darken the doors of a concert hall, but she could curl up in the comfort of a friend's home and be sung over by her heavenly Father.

Beloved, this is our God-propelled capacity at its finest. I love how the landscape of Whitney's small-town ministry is reaching all the way to you, to encourage you even now. It reminds me of Jesus and His small-town ministry. I seem to recall a group of friends who carried their friend to Jesus, lowering him down into the home where Jesus was teaching and healing. By the way, I've seen the house where archaeologists believe this happened. It's *tiny*. Living inside out can actually keep us on the edge of *our* seats, wondering how God might show up next in the smallness of our lives.

What I love about the kingdom of God is that it's always been inside out and upside down from what we're used to. Including the fact that what's seemingly big is really small and what's seemingly small is really big. Jesus said that in heaven, those who have been first here on earth will be last and those who have been last will be first.[2] He also considered small acts of kindness, such as a cup of cold water offered to a thirsty child, as a ministry that would reap a lasting reward.[3] Jesus lived out from the infinitely gigantic story of His Father's love—but it had the look and feel of small-town life, even keeping close quarters with these brothers He loved.

I wonder if we can get so caught up in building the next big thing that we insulate ourselves from the most important things in life. We build up cultures and perceptions and require others to align with the way we prefer things to look and feel. Soon, we're not able to see beyond the borders of the bubbles we've created. We have neighborhood bubbles, church bubbles, private school bubbles, ministry bubbles—you name it. Inside, it might feel like the biggest and best thing going, but from the outside in, it looks a little bit like a snow globe—pretty and magical at first glance but disconcertingly closed off from real life.

What if we began to rest from the pressure and expectation to build big things and instead lived our normal-sized lives with great expectancy centered on *the* big thing—our Father's heart? We don't have to let our conditioned Western mindset measure the worth of who we are and what we're about by what we're building. Nor should we ever have to apologize or give a disclaimer for being about the small things. Remember, God is the one building us, and He's got the *whole* globe in His hands!

There's another small but stout Greek word that I want you to know about. It's the word *teleios,* and it means "complete."[4] The root of this word (*tel*) means "reaching the end (aim)." This idea suggests "the old pirate's telescope, unfolding (extending out) one stage at a time to function at full-strength (capacity effectiveness)."[5] If we pair this with the other tiny-but-mighty Greek word *ek* ("out from"), we could imagine ourselves being this old pirate's telescope. Can't you just see us now, allowing ourselves to collapse all the way down into the bullseye of God's heart to rest and then emerging out from Him each day to full capacity, strength, and effectiveness by His Spirit in us?

This might blow your mind a little, but did you know that when Scripture says to "be perfect as your heavenly Father is perfect," it's translated from this word *teleios*?[6] If you're like me, you've read that verse before and saw it to be so unattainable, so unreachable that you kind of just shoved it under a rug with a few other things you don't know what to do with. But what hope this offers us! That to be perfect is to be able to extend out, one stage at a time, from the perfection of our Father, to our fullest capacity! Beloved, this is no small thing.

GO DEEP

I have a vivid memory of standing in front of my bathroom mirror one frigid winter afternoon, wondering to myself if it was really going to matter whether I showed up to lead worship that night for a nearby event I was scheduled for. I was also trying to assess how much adrenaline I needed to muster to make my face and hair look like something other than they did. I sighed, knowing I needed to kick things into another gear if I was not going to be late. There were already loads of weather advisories out for possible freezing rain. I thought to myself, *Will anyone even be there?* I was giving up on the night before it had even started. Right then, a clear and direct thought filled my mind:

Keep digging deep wells.

Sometimes when the Holy Spirit whispers, it's as if He speaks volumes through only a few small words. I immediately thought about some of the small but deeply meaningful ministry moments that I had been a part of lately, and I pictured a deep well in each place. I thought about small and unseen ministry moments over the past twenty years and imagined deep wells there too. My family, my marriage, and my children—each of them represented a deep and lasting well.

Jesus was pulling things back into focus. I didn't need to feel weighted down with the pressure to go wide or worry about how far-reaching that night would be. I just needed to plant my feet firmly where God had called me and dig deep. My job was to offer the depth of Jesus without apology and to trust that He had something to impart to those people that was bigger than anything that I could bring.

When I got to the church, it seemed as if the same nagging lie of smallness and insignificance had been discouraging my band members all day. We huddled up, and I shared with them how God encouraged my heart to keep digging deep wells, even when what we're doing seems meaningless and unseen.

With a renewed sense of purpose, we took the stage together, determined to bring our best, whether worshipping with ten people or ten thousand. I made a conscious choice that this moment mattered and that we were not there to just sing songs. We were there to excavate beyond the surface and believe that God would meet us there in a powerful way.

The crowd wasn't huge, but I will say, it was decent for an icy Valentine's night. We started our worship set in a not-so-flashy way. While everyone was still seated, I centered my heart and believed it louder than I could sing it: "I'm coming back to the heart of worship, and it's all about You, Jesus."[7] An elderly man in about the third row stood up, stretched his arms as high as he could toward the heavens, and began to sing with me. The atmosphere began to shift throughout the entire room, and something beautiful broke open as people began to stand to their feet and follow his lead. Before the night was over, people were kneeling throughout the room, weeping, praying, and meeting with God. It was a night I'll never forget.

Maybe you've become weary of small. Trust me, I get it. But can I encourage you to not give up on the deep? Maybe you find yourself deeply engrossed in toddler talk all day, with littles who seem to be permanently attached to your hip. I assure you, you're going to reap what you sow. I can't tell you how grateful I am that God got ahold of my heart when my kids were little and helped me see the big, bright, beautiful ministry of getting to be their mama. I truly fear that I would have missed it if not for God's grace! What a joy it is to know my children and get to converse with them now about meaningful matters of the heart. Keep it up, Mama. It's going to be worth it!

Maybe you know deep down that God has called you to a meaningful ministry right where you are, but you've become distracted and discouraged by the next big thing in town because it feels like direct competition. It's already hard enough pulling things together with a shoestring budget and a mustard seed of faith! Keep digging deep wells, friend. Keep your eyes on Jesus, and love the people around you well. That's the stuff of eternity!

If you're buried beneath a pile of work in a cubicle today, a kind of small that you expected to move beyond years ago, stay the course and be faithful right where you are. You have a globe-holding God who loves you and sees what's done in secret. He will reward you!

I like to think that our kingdom impact goes wide by our leaving countless deep wells wherever we go. Wells that become vital gathering places in our hometowns or in our neighborhoods. The kind that beckon people to go out of their way to come taste and see the goodness of God. The kind that end up being a lasting source of life for generations to come.

MONUMENTALLY SMALL

Another unforgettable vantage point in Israel was looking out over the Lower Galilee from about six hundred feet above it, on the top of Mount Arbel. I know, six hundred feet doesn't sound like a very big mountain. That's because it's not! In America, we would call it a cliff. Even Shai acknowledged the peculiarity that, in Israel, lakes are called seas and cliffs and hills are called mountains. (Sidenote: The Scriptures don't mention that Jesus spent time on Mount Arbel, but I can't fathom that He didn't. If you could experience the view, you'd probably wonder, like me, if this is where Jesus often retreated alone to the hills to pray.) While it's not the highest peak in Israel, it is the most prominent hill in the lower region of Galilee, giving one a spectacular view of where Jesus truly lived His life.

I can just picture Him up there praying over His Beloved community. You can see Capernaum, a village where He lived, from that peak as well as many other towns where we know He spent time. You can see almost the entire Sea of Galilee, where He first met the fisherman friends He'd soon call brothers and disciples. And there in the foothills, right in front of us, sat gorgeous Magdala, Mary Magdalene's hometown. We'd later get to explore it in detail, including a first-century synagogue that was only unearthed in 2009. Scholars are certain that Jesus would have taught there. It was of course breathtakingly small.

As we looked out over that gorgeous land that morning, our American guide, Cary, pointed out why our view was particularly significant. This is because we could see with our eyes the landscape of Jesus's earthly ministry. Excluding His journeys to Jerusalem, Jesus's main ministry all happened within about a twenty-seven-mile radius. In just three years, within that relatively short distance, Jesus changed the world. Talk about the power of *small*.

Jesus's scale of ministry was all about big things in small places and small things in big places. He noticed and healed the sick lying near the vast public pools, outcasts who had become like permanent fixtures of the landscape. He saw the widow's tiny offering in the temple that day, as she gave her all. He acknowledged out loud the power He felt leave Him when a woman touched just the hem of His robe for healing. He remained quiet when everyone thought He should have piped up and made His voice known when they least expected it. After some of His most miraculous moments, He instructed those around Him to "tell no one."[8]

It dawned on me how important it is to read the Bible, as best we can, within the framework and context of what life was really like in that time. If not, we're liable to place our supersized, unrealistic, and even unreachable expectations on the commands the Lord has given us. We might give up before we've even begun and completely miss His beautiful invitation into His statutes, which are actually His blessings.

As we looked out on Jesus's neighborhood that morning, from the hills He most likely knew well, Cary prompted us to consider Jesus's answer when asked to name the most important of all the commandments: "You shall love the Lord your God with all your heart and with all your soul and with all your mind. This is the great and first commandment. And a second is like it: You shall love your neighbor as yourself. On these two commandments depend all the Law and the Prophets."[9]

Kind of sounds like bullseye living, doesn't it? I also think that it shows us that Jesus's call for us to live *out from* the love of the Father and *to* the world around us isn't just a sidenote. It is the strategy, the driving principle, of His kingdom. He meant this as a serious means of ministry that would change the world. He proved it by living it. Out from His Father's heart, in a small corner of His Father's world, He loved His neighbors and changed the course of history.

Beloved, my prayer is that this makes your corner of the world feel suddenly monumental and potentially miraculous. May you consider that the den of your humble abode could be a grand concert hall. May you notice and reach out to the permanent fixtures of your landscape—the community that God is no doubt bringing into the general vicinity of *you*.

The next time you stand in your God-propelled capacity, may you consider the truth that by His Spirit you are taking ground and digging a deep, life-giving well that will last! May you embrace and value and even rest in what God has called you to, even if it seems small. Jesus *gets* small. I think He finds it gloriously familiar.

You need not wander far to find the life you long for, Beloved.

Welcome home!

FOR REFLECTION OR DISCUSSION

1. What's the difference between feeling pressure to build big things yourself and expecting God to build big things? What does that difference look like when it comes to your daily decisions and relationships?

   _____

   _____

   _____

   _____

2. What "small" act of service or love might God be calling you to today?

   _____

   _____

   _____

   _____

3. In what ways did Jesus's earthly ministry contrast with the values of our contemporary culture?

   _____

   _____

   _____

   _____

12

—

ALWAYS REMEMBER
TO NEVER FORGET

LITTLE GIRLS HAVE A YEARNING AND A LONGING THAT we don't often speak of, even when we're not so little anymore. We don't always recognize this longing. It just rises in the form of questions when we look in the mirror each morning with a wince and wonder, *Is what I have to offer of any worth?*

I remember when these questions started to form in my daughters' minds and hearts. It happened long before I was ready, as it seems to confront little girls younger than ever these days. When they were about eight and thirteen, I decided to sit them down and just go there with calling out the longing as I asked, "When you look in the mirror, do you ever ask yourself questions?"

Now wincing at me, they seemed puzzled as to how I knew about the questions.

I continued to prod, asking if when they saw their reflections, did they ever wonder things like *Am I beautiful? Am I worth anything in this world?* Looking slightly mortified but fascinated, they nodded their heads yes. I brought up the name of their favorite actress at the time and blew their minds by telling them that she, no doubt, wakes up every morning asking herself the same things. I assured them that the only reason I knew about the questions is because I ask them too.

Carefully looking each of them in the eyes, I declared, "I want you to hear it from me, right here and right now: the answer is *yes.* Yes, you are beautiful and your value and your worth are utterly priceless." They shyly grinned and beamed, believing it in that moment. But oh, how easy it is to forget!

Later that afternoon, I shared this defining moment with my husband and what a privilege it was to speak life-giving words into our daughters' hearts, face to face. At the time, we were writing for our lullaby album, so naturally he said, "This needs to be a song!"

He recalled a saying that he's used with the kids over the years, especially when he'd walk into the house from his peaceful workplace only to be met with the three-ring circus that was me trying to mother and manage our home. (He didn't say the circus part, but that is certainly how I felt most days when the kids were little!) When he'd see that I was on the verge of losing it, he'd give this little dad whistle. All three kids would freeze and look up. When the room was quiet, he'd say, "Always remember"—he'd pause, leaving them hanging for a second and then resolve it by saying—"to never forget!" This was his quirky but witty way of resetting the temperature of the room when I was all out of tries.

In the days that followed my conversation with our girls, we wrote a song to speak truth into the hallowed space of that longing. It's musically a waltz, and I imagine little girls everywhere feeling invited to dance as the song rings out:

> Always remember to never forget,
> When you look in the mirror
> The answer is yes—
> Yes, you are pure as gold,
> Yes, you are beautiful;
> So always remember to never forget!
>
> My darling, you're like His favorite parade on a bright,
>   sunny day
> In the middle of the mossy forest you'll dance
> In your favorite dress,
> And oh, how He loves when you never forget![1]

I can't help but think about how much we bless God when we remember. Remembrance is essential to thriving from a soul-settling rest. A life of trust in God is choosing to remember His life-altering Word—to renew our minds with what is true of Him and true of us.[2] My brother Eric, who's always thinking outside the box, has helped me to see that the quiet time that we become is really a time of remembrance, isn't it? Instead of a box to check off our spiritual to-do list, what if we told our souls each day, *It's time to go remember.* This is what will set our lives and our songs and our dances apart from the world—when we become the remembering ones.

As this book comes to a close, I find myself wishing I

could look you right in the eyes—so that you can hear it from someone who really believes it on your behalf—and say, "Yes. Yes, you are beautiful, and what you have to offer is of unspeakable worth—you're priceless." I hope you've heard me being honest with you, just as I am with myself and my children, about who you really are. Chances are, you already knew before you picked up this book, but it seems that none of us ever outgrows the need to be reminded. Maybe life has started to look like that three-ring circus and you just needed your Father to come in and whistle and be the lifter of your head again—to remember that the most vital thing is to look to Him and to hang on His every word.

QUESTIONS TO HELP YOU REMEMBER WHAT MATTERS

As we noted early on in this book, some of life's greatest answers come in the form of questions. Not only do questions help us get to the heart of the matter, but they also help us to keep remembering the heart of the matter.

Do you remember the five Ws of journalism, the ones you probably learned in grade school? These were the questions we were told to use in gathering information about whatever we were researching or studying. Somewhere along the way, the question *how* was added, so they became the five Ws and an H.

With that as my inspiration, I give you the seven wonders of the Beloved: who, whose, when, where, how, what, and why. Yes, mine are a little bit different because I like to be different. Plus I have a thing for sevens. In any case, I hope these prodding answers—in the form of questions—help you *always remember to never forget.*

Who Are You, Beloved?

This world is going to look you in the eyes and feed you the line that "you are enough." While it might sound inspirational and maybe even loving, please don't take the bait. You and I both know that our own strength and enoughness are going to tucker out at some point.

If you have trusted Christ with your life, you bear the highest calling of being God's Beloved child. And herein lies the secret to true heart rest: surrender your life to live from the enoughness of Christ. In surrendering your own self-sufficiency, what do you stand to gain? Endless sufficiency. Paul gave us some inspiration to build our lives on when he reminded us that God's grace is sufficient—more than enough for us—and His power is even made perfect in our weakness.[3]

Here's that word *perfect* again. As I'm sure you guessed, it comes from that Greek word *teleios,* with the root meaning "to function at full-strength (capacity effectiveness)."[4] The contrasting word *weakness* can be defined as "want of strength" or "illness, suffering, calamity, frailty."[5] I don't know about you, but I want to find my worth wrapped up in the One who meets me right where I am, in every season, and even causes His power to extend out of my weakest moments in life. How beautiful is it that God's life can flow through us in our fullest capacity, just as His fullest capacity can flow through our weakest frailty?

Even though it may seem like silly semantics, *who* we are as the Beloved will forever be found and intrinsically tied to *whose* we are.

Whose Are You, Beloved?

You were made in the image of the most beautiful and valuable Being there is—and you belong to Him! You were knit together with purpose, to reflect who God is to the world around you.[6]

Another undeniable aspect of whose we are is that you and I belong to each other.[7] Several years ago I stood next to my sister-in-law Kristin at a large gathering for women. We looked around, in awe of the sheer number of women who had turned up to learn how to disciple the next generation. Knowing all that she was carrying in that season and having an up-close view of all that I carry, she said to me, "You know, it's important that we get arm in arm together as women and remember that we are running a relay in this life, not a sprint." She elaborated, "What if instead of feeling the constant pressure to run at full capacity, we take turns?" Just then, the woman leading from stage asked the entire room to link arms together as we prayed. Kristin and I smiled at each other as it felt like our own little confirmation of what she had just shared.

This is the beauty of the community of the Beloved. We link arms and look out for each other. We stay engaged in such a way that we know whose turn it is to run and whose turn it is to rest. And those who are running can run from rest because we are helping to hold up their causes! Before we move on to the *what* and the *why* of our lives each day, we get to cherish first the people that God has entrusted to us. Instead of leaving them behind, we bring them with us into what we are called to as God's Beloved.

Whatever provision you seek today, practice giving that very provision away to those around you. If you need encouragement, be intentional in encouraging others and see if God won't give back a hundredfold what you pour into your Beloved community.

When Is Your Time, Beloved?

Seasons come and go, and as we discussed earlier, unexpected life changes sometimes look like hitting oil and struggling for stability. I remember when Nathan and I both sensed that God was bringing our season in Atlanta to an end—actually asking us to step away from a ministry that we had served for twenty years, one that had shaped our belief in God's story like nothing else had. As I lamented the change, some days I'd sit with my forehead leaning on the upright piano in our foyer, imagining myself leaning on Jesus. I'd sing through the last sliver of sunlight, as my fingers found the familiar chords beneath them. This was a comfort when nothing else seemed familiar and the sun was setting on an entire chapter of our lives.

The thing is, just when we think we've found our forever, Jesus always seems to call us onward! As the Beloved, we can know that our appointed time is always today.[8] Through every high and every low, let us not harden our hearts toward God but choose to enter the rest that He has given us in Christ

Jesus, *today*. Living our gospel story beyond our salvation, obeying and trusting Him even in the mystery, and being ready in and out of season for all He has called us to. When you trust Jesus and obey Him, especially when a season is ending, you can be assured that the moment marks the beginning of the rest of your life!

Where Are You, Beloved?

One rainy afternoon when our youngest, Annie Rose, was inching toward three years old, we got out some home videos of when the kids were younger to keep them entertained. Annie Rose sat perfectly still, sucking those two fingers of hers. She was completely mesmerized to see herself as an infant, as we kept pointing out, "There's baby Annie Rose!"

A couple of hours later, out of nowhere, she asked me, "Mommy, where *is* I'm?" I tried to grasp what she was saying while also trying not to laugh, as she said it again with fervor, "Where *is* I'm?" I assured her that she was right there with me, but she quickly whined, "No, where is *baby* Annie Rose?"

I suddenly realized that she hadn't put two and two together that baby Annie Rose from the video was herself! I think she was so taken with that cuddly, cute baby that she wanted to know where to find her! I said, "She's you! *You* are baby Annie Rose, but you are growing up and getting bigger!" She smiled at me bashfully as we both sat there and giggled.

We talk so much about who we are in Christ, but it's not often that we think about the reality of *where* we are in Christ.

My mom taught me a beautiful illustration years ago, which she learned from her author friend Anabel Gillham. On a sidenote, Anabel—who is Home with Jesus now—was someone who devoted her life to helping people understand who they are in Christ. I feel a little less odd when I read some of her hands-on illustrations and how she so often used her spiritual imagination to lead herself and others well in trusting God. Things like writing a letter to God in which you cast on Him (rather than carry) whatever your specific burden is. Then you sign it and seal it and date the outside of the envelope and keep it somewhere to remind yourself that you've given that burden over to Him.

A big part of my learning to live from a heart of rest has been learning to use my spiritual imagination. Hence my habit of hiding underneath my covers! Before you get weirded out by this, using your spiritual imagination is really the same thing as living out your faith. Faith that God is who He says He is and that you are who and where He says you are. Again, I'm just trying to shake things up a little because I think sometimes we see familiar words like *faith* and we start to zone out. I'm not suggesting that you play mind games in order to believe in God, but I am saying that we have a choice in what we choose to dwell on! If sealing up in an envelope what we've cast on the Lord helps us remember to rest in what He's carrying on our behalf, why wouldn't we?

That goes for this envelope exercise too. If my husband, Nathan, could interject right here, he'd warn you that you have now entered Christy's Craft Corner and that you might want to run to your local craft store to pick up some supplies!

But maybe for now, just use that spiritual imagination of yours for what can later be a more hands-on picture of where you are as the Beloved of God. I've taken some creative liberties with Anabel's basic idea.[9]

Gather three envelopes of graduated sizes—small, medium, and large—as well as a slip of paper and a bit of decorative tape, such as washi tape. You can embellish the envelopes and make them pretty and Pinterest-worthy if you want, or you can just go Office Depot style. You do you!

On the largest envelope, print "The Father." On the next size envelope, print "Christ Jesus." On the smallest of the three envelopes, print your name. And on the little slip of paper, print "Christ Jesus" again.

After you've done this, take the slip of paper with "Christ Jesus" on it and place it inside the envelope with your name on it. Beloved, Christ is in you![10] Now, take that envelope with your name on it, with "Christ Jesus" inside, and place it inside the larger envelope that says "Christ Jesus." Christ is in you, but you are also in Christ![11] How amazing is that?

Next, take the "Christ Jesus" envelope and place it inside the largest envelope that says "The Father." Beloved, this is *where* you are! Christ is in you and you are in Christ and He is in the Father. This is what Jesus meant when He said in John 14:20, "In that day you will know that I am in my Father, and you in me, and I in you."

Now, use your decorative tape to seal this outer envelope and write "The Holy Spirit" across the tape. It is true that the Spirit of God is in you,[12] and He is also the blessed seal that covers where you are in Christ! Ephesians 1:13 says, "In him you also, when you heard the word of truth, the gospel of your salvation, and believed in him, were sealed with the promised Holy Spirit."

Beloved, you are hidden within this magnificent mystery of our three-in-one God! Resting within those envelopes is your true reality, your very identity, and the life you long for. Think about it: anything that happens to us must first go through the Father and through Christ. And because Christ is in us by His Spirit, we are covered by the great Comforter as well as filled with the peace that only He can give. Why should we be afraid?

I rested underneath this covering as I waited over two months to see a neurosurgeon about the mystery spot that the MRI found on my brain during my hearing-loss saga. It helped me wait in quiet trust, knowing that God was with me in the waiting and that the outcome was enveloped in His divine covering. I'm happy to tell you that the neurosurgeon confirmed that the spot on my brain was just a benign cyst that I was probably born with. My friend Emily teased me that it's just my extra little something that God gave me to pull from when I need an extra little something!

One of the last times that I gathered those lovely worship leader women in my Georgia home, before we made our way back to Tennessee, my heart was aching. I knew deep down how much I would miss their big, bright, beautiful hearts. I made them each a set of these envelopes of remembrance, after I battled the lie that they would think it was elementary and irrelevant.

It actually brought a holy hush over the room as they opened their personalized envelopes of where they are in Christ. I left each of the envelopes unsealed so that they could reach into the mystery of God, right there in my den, and experience the covering of His love. My hope was to help them remember not only that nothing can touch them unless it goes through the Father, the Son, and the Holy Spirit but also that this three-in-one God can powerfully live *through* them, changing everything they touch in this life!

How Will You Endure, Beloved?

First of all, to endure is no small thing. It's tied to that longevity I mentioned earlier, the staying power to remain and last, preserving our faith and trust in God to the end of our days. My hope is that by this point in the book, your mind went straight to the truth that we don't have staying power in and of ourselves. We, as the Beloved, are "strengthened with all power, according to *his* glorious might, for all endurance and patience *with* joy."[13] The word *endurance* here in the Greek means an enabling to "remain under."[14] I can't help but think about that big banner of God's love over us and how He's called us to come underneath it and live out from it.

It's also no small thing that we are called to remain under God's love together, as the Beloved. As we stay "grounded in [God's] love," we will be able to experience "together with all the saints" what is the "length and width and height and depth of the love of Christ" and "the fullness of God."[15]

What a promise! That we get to endure *together* and that we were made to experience, shoulder to shoulder, the fullness of God's love. No wonder Satan loves to stir the pot of dissension and disunity within the church! If he can get us backstabbing and bickering, sometimes that's all it takes to completely derail an entire community. It's vital that we stay awake to this and understand who the real Enemy is when we are experiencing trouble within our church and community.

Sometimes the Enemy lures us to step out from underneath God's banner of love and operate instead out of our own small love, where we tend to lean on our own agendas. We think we can outlove God by getting up in everyone else's business, certain we know what's best for all. Like the times I've tried to fix things by force, strapping on that "it's all up to me" backpack and becoming my own defender and even the defender of others. I've even puffed up with pride and tried to defend the church before, as if God didn't have the situation under control!

All the Enemy has to do is draw us into outer-ring living again, and before long we'll have worn out our welcome. We'll lose the joy in welcoming others into our familiar with the Father. Beloved, along with guarding our hearts, we must guard our welcome.

My welcome was pretty beat up and tattered in the months leading up to my fortieth birthday. One evening the kids and I were sitting in a family-friendly little Irish pub down the street from our house. Nathan was out of town and we were missing him, so we had decided to head to our favorite dinner spot to pass the time. While the kids chatted with each other and bounced around in the booth, a section of a mural on the wall caught my eye. I've always heard people say things like "This image really spoke to me," and that's the best way I know how to describe it. I just wasn't sure yet how it was speaking to me!

It's a print of a painting set in what looks like the fifteenth century, and it portrays a man and a woman standing in a close embrace. The woman's countenance is radiant with rest. Her eyes are closed and her head is buried in the man's chest, so close that she can't see his expression. And that's what gets me every time: his expression. He's strong and noble, dressed in armor with his sword at his side, but his eyes are closed as he gently kisses the top of her head. The first time I saw it, I thought to myself, *He's engaged in the embrace.* Isn't that every woman's dream? He doesn't have his eyes set on his next task or the journey ahead. He's present, right there with her, even savoring her in the moment. I couldn't take my eyes off the image, and the kids were finally like "Mom, just take a picture!"

The following days, I'd find myself peering repeatedly at the image on my phone. I showed it to Nathan when he got home, explaining that something about it spoke to me deeply, but I wasn't sure yet what it was. I don't know why I waited so long to simply ask the Lord. When I did, the significance became crystal clear to me. This was a picture of a bride-groom and his bride, but the Lord made it plain that for me it represented Christ and His church.

I determined that if God was showing me a picture of Christ and His church, then He was certainly still engaged in the embrace. This encouraged my heart that He had not abandoned her or forsaken her, but He was still holding on to her with a look of love on His face. As I examined further, I could clearly see His strength and valor. She didn't need my defending after all. He was her defender. And that's when the Holy Spirit seemed to move in close to whisper, *She's you. Take your place in the embrace.*

My eyes began to burn with tears as I felt my defensive posture give way to rest. Jesus was making it clear to me that to endure as His Beloved, I simply needed to settle into His embrace again, because His love endures forever.[16] I needed to run back to His welcome to find my own.

The weekend of my fortieth birthday rolled around, and Nathan took me away to a beautiful inn in North Carolina. A fire was lit in our room to welcome and warm us on that crisp, autumn night. The setting was picturesque. As I walked through the door of the bedroom, I stopped in my tracks. There, hanging on the wall in our room, was the image from the pub! I looked at Nathan, and he appeared to be as shocked as I felt. We both walked over to it. My heart was pounding, knowing that God must really want to drive this message home to me! I squealed out loud as I saw that the artist had signed the framed print. This meant that I could maybe track it down on the internet and own one of my own!

As I squinted to try to make out the artist's name, Nathan leaned in close and whispered, "Happy birthday." It took me a good minute to realize what was going on. Nathan explained that for weeks he had been searching for that image and finally found it *and* the guy who painted it. Apparently, no prints of it were available. But Nathan told him the whole story, and the artist decided to print one just for us and even signed it. Nathan took the kids with him to have it framed and then shipped it ahead of time to the inn where we'd be staying. Just before our arrival, the people at the inn graciously removed the picture that normally hangs in that bedroom and replaced it with this precious gift.

Beloved, God will go to great lengths to reveal places in

our hearts that He's not done fighting for. This is because He knows full well that the hallowed space of our longing is a space that only He can fill. He also knows that when we allow Him to fill that space in us, we will be propelled out from His rest into the *what* and *why* that He has prepared for us.

What Are the What and the Why, Beloved?

You may remember that I told you way back in chapter 4 that the *what* and the *why* of our lives really do matter. The secret is to approach them in the right order. Living from who and whose we are pinpoints, propels, and protects what we are called to. As you live out from loving God with all your heart, mind, and soul and loving your neighbor as yourself, I believe that not only will you begin living the life you long for but you'll also long for the life that *God* longs for.

You'll be postured to carry out the small but mighty strategy for fulfilling the Great Commission—the revolutionary charge from our resurrected Lord that led to you and me becoming the Beloved of God! From the top of a mountain in Galilee, maybe even from the peak of the small but mighty Mount Arbel, Jesus said to His eleven disciples,

> All authority in heaven and on earth has been given to me. Go therefore and make disciples of all nations, baptizing them in the name of the Father and of the Son and of the Holy Spirit, teaching them to observe all that I have commanded you. And behold, I am with you always, to the end of the age.[17]

And from His tiny corner of the world to ours, He affirmed the *what* of the Beloved: that out from God we get to re-present Christ to the world, welcoming others into our familiar with Him.

What is the *why,* you ask? The answer to our why is found in the One who knows that some of life's best answers are questions.

When Jesus turned and saw two men following, He asked them, "What do you want?"

They replied, "Where are you staying?"

"Come and see," He said.[18]

In living from our Belovedness, our *why* in this life is always and only Jesus. Because the life we long for and the rest we need is forever found wherever He is.

FOR REFLECTION OR DISCUSSION

1. Why is it freeing to realize we are not enough?

_____

_____

_____

_____

2. What do you most want to remember from this book? Why?

_____

_____

_____

_____

3. Think back to how you described the life you long for at the beginning of the book. Has your answer changed at all? If so, how?

_____

_____

_____

_____

ACKNOWLEDGMENTS

God, thank You for meeting me in the mystery on the back porch of the old house in Muskogee. I must have been six or seven, as memories of mud pies with yellow dandelion "icing" come to mind. I'm forever grateful that somehow, even then, I knew You and that You were coming after my heart.

Thank You for rescuing me from *me* when I got older and thought I knew better. For fighting for my heart even when I unknowingly fought against You—armed with all that I thought I was supposed to be doing *for* You. Thank You for giving me just enough of what I thought I wanted so that I could discover what it is that I truly need. And thank You for grace upon grace to keep finding that You are my portion and the life I long for. All of this is for You but, most important, *from* You.

Nathan, my husband of twenty-five years, the one I've been living (and defining) the dream with since I was nineteen. It's *still* a joy to make meaningful music with you after all this time! Thank you for leading the charge on working from rest and modeling the family-first agenda. You are reaping what you've sown as a husband and a father, choosing all these years to be present at the dinner table and the kids' bedtime routine. No one on earth has believed in me more than you, and no one has paved the way for this book like you have. Thank you for the countless hours you steadied the ship so this message could come forth. *I love you dearly.*

To my beautiful and brilliant children, Noah, Elliana, and Annie Rose. I never saw it coming—how mothering you, knowing you, *loving* you, and singing over you would change my life forever. You taught me how to be a child of God again! I treasure you, and home will forever be wherever you are!

Mom and Dad, Susan and Lynn Hill. I wanted to print your names because, yes, you've been my parents, but you're also people who have lived this life-changing, beauty-from-ashes story that Christ is *enough*. Your trust and rest in God have helped shape my life's song, and this book is only some of the fruit of your incredible prayer life together! *Thank you!*

Eric and Kristin Hill, when I think of the two of you, I think of Jesus. Thank you for literally spending your lives helping people like me remember and rest in who He is and what He has *already* done!

Kay and Dennis Nockels, thank you for all the times you've stormed heaven on our behalf and, Kay, for the texts that encourage my artist heart!

Matt Guice, my manager and friend! Nate and I are so grateful to God for you. We wouldn't be where we are without you. Your and Rachael's belief in us means the world, and it's a joy to get to re-present Christ alongside you!

Curtis and Karen Yates, I couldn't have (and maybe wouldn't have) ever done this without you. You stuck with me through five years of spiritually squirming around the idea of writing a book! Your pastoral hearts and friendship have made this process incredibly and unexpectedly life giving. Thank you for taking a huge risk on me and for championing this message of rest!

Laura Barker, your kindness, wisdom, patience (and prayer over the phone when I needed it) have marked me and made me better and brought this message to life! Even when my writing felt like throwing things against the wall to see what would stick, you stuck with me! You have challenged and championed me in a beautiful way—for every edit, you sent *edification*—and I'm forever grateful!

Lauren Chandler, God would have gotten my attention one way or another, but I'm *so* glad He chose to use you, beautiful friend! I'm ever grateful for how you live out from God and trust His Word. You are stunning!

Beth Moore, thank you for having eyes to see a twenty-three-year-old girl just starting out. You've always spoken truth into my heart, and you've even shared your platform, but most important, you've mothered us all so well by taking your place in the embrace of Jesus!

Teri Price, your spiritual mama heart changed my life forever! Thank you for *seeing* me and for speaking the life that Jesus offers into my exhausted heart.

Jennie Allen. Thank you, friend, for all the times on tour when you saw me *still* writing this book in the back of the bus, and you clapped your hands and said, "I'm so proud of you, Christy. You can do this!"

Thank you to the Beloved community of women who have listened to me, prayed for me, and lifted me all along the way: Whitney Prosperi, Molley Moody, Joanna Weaver, Shannon Scott, Lauren Tomlin, Magen Roberson, Meshali Mitchell, Rebekah Lyons, Jody Campbell, Melinda Mayton, Brittany Batson, Margaret Feinberg, Suzanne Phillips, Annie Downs, and Kristin Cline.

Seth Haines, thank you for the book-mapping day with Karen that created space for God to restore some places in my heart so that I could actually *write* this book. Also, thanks to Brent Cole for your incredible input that helped me find the spark to just get started. And to Dr. Brian Russell for being gracious to answer my long email about Psalm 37!

To the patrons of *The Glorious in the Mundane* podcast and all those who have helped launch this book. Thank you, Beloved community, for your prayer and support and for championing this message of heart rest alongside me! I'm forever grateful!

To the Multnomah team: Tina, Campbell, Laura B., Bev, Ginia, Johanna, Lisa, Andrea, Lori, Todd, Cynthia, Laura W., Leslie, and Levi. I'll never forget sitting around the table at DFW with several of you and being blown away by your hearts and your investment in me and this message being delivered to the Beloved! Your calling, community, and capacity have inspired me, as I can clearly see that you care deeply about God's Word and helping people to *trust* Him and live *from* Him. Thank you for being willing to take a huge risk on a brand-new author and for patiently leading me as I learn!

NOTES

Chapter 1: His Banner over Me Is Love

1. 1 John 3:1–3; 1 John 4:7–8; Ephesians 5:1–2; HELPS Word-studies, s.v. "27 *agapētos*," Bible Hub, 2011, https://biblehub.com/greek/27.htm.
2. Andrew Murray, *Abiding in Christ* (Minneapolis: Bethany House, 2003), 25.
3. Ephesians 6:12.
4. Hebrews 9:15.
5. John 1:38–39, NLT.

Part 1: The Calling of the Beloved

1. 1 John 3:1.
2. 2 Corinthians 7:1; Colossians 3:17.
3. Matthew 11:28–30.
4. *Strong's Lexicon,* s.v. "Come," Matthew 11:28, Bible Hub, https://biblehub.com/parallel/matthew/11-28.htm.

Chapter 2: The Farm-Table Epiphany

1. Matthew 7:17, NIV.
2. Romans 8:15.
3. Psalm 37:4, NLT.
4. *Strong's Concordance,* s.v. *"nathan,"* Bible Hub, https://biblehub .com/hebrew/5414.htm.
5. Psalm 37:5, NLT.
6. Isaiah 64:6, NLT.
7. Acts 2:28.
8. John 16:33.
9. Jeremiah 17:5–8.
10. Philippians 2:3–4.
11. Ephesians 2:10.

Chapter 3: The Glorious in the Mundane

1. Jennifer Garner, *13 Going on 30,* directed by Gary Winick (New York: Sony Pictures Entertainment, 2004), IMDb, www.imdb .com/title/tt0337563/quotes.
2. Matthew 18:1–4.
3. "18:2–4 Whoever humbles himself like this child," *ESV Study Bible* (Wheaton, IL: Crossway, 2008), 1858.
4. John 15:5.
5. Matthew 10:39.
6. Colossians 1:27.
7. Dr. and Mrs. Howard Taylor, *Hudson Taylor's Spiritual Secret* (Chicago: Moody, 2009), 159.
8. *Brown-Driver-Briggs Hebrew and English Lexicon,* s.v. *"chalaph,"* Bible Hub, 2006, https://biblehub.com/hebrew/2498.htm.
9. Psalm 1:3, NIV.

Chapter 4: The Already of Our Story

1. HELPS Word-studies, s.v. "1537 *ek,"* Bible Hub, 2011, https:// biblehub.com/greek/1537.htm.
2. Maxie Dunnam, *The Intercessory Life* (Wilmore, KY: Seedbed, 2013), 95.
3. Colossians 3:12, NIV.
4. 2 Corinthians 12:9.

5. Colossians 3, ESV, NIV.

6. Romans 8:5–6.

7. Luke 10:27.

8. Exodus 6:7.

9. Christopher Ash, *Bible Delight: Heartbeat of the Word of God: Psalm 119 for the Bible Teacher and Hearer* (Fearn, Scotland: Christian Focus Publications; and London: Proclamation Trust Media, 2014), 36.

10. 1 John 5:3.

11. Eric and Kristin Hill, *The First Breakfast* (Milton, GA: With You Ministries, 2019), 18–19.

Chapter 5: Those Who Look to Him

1. Psalm 43:5.

2. Psalm 103:1.

3. 1 Thessalonians 5:23.

4. *Strong's Concordance,* s.v. *"nephesh,"* Bible Hub, https://biblehub.com/hebrew/5315.htm.

5. John 8:44; Revelation 12:9–10; Ephesians 2:2.

6. Romans 8:5, MSG.

7. Romans 8:5–6, MSG.

8. Romans 8:6.

9. 2 Corinthians 10:4.

10. Galatians 4:6.

11. Ephesians 1:13–14.

12. Ezekiel 36:26.

13. Jeremiah 24:7.

14. 2 Corinthians 3:3; Hebrews 10:16.

15. Colossians 2:13, NIV; Romans 8:7.

16. 2 Corinthians 5:17.

17. Galatians 2:20; Romans 6:4.

18. Ephesians 2:6.

19. 1 John 4:4.

20. Bill Gillham, *Lifetime Guarantee* (Eugene, OR: Harvest House, 1993), 136–37.

21. Romans 7:4.

22. 2 Corinthians 10:5.

23. 2 Thessalonians 3:6–12; Colossians 3:23–24.

24. Psalm 34:5, NIV.

25. A. W. Tozer, *The Pursuit of God (The Definitive Classic)*, ed. James L. Snyder (Ventura, CA: Regal, 2013), 82.

26. Tozer, *Pursuit of God*, 86.

27. Revelation 7:9.

28. 1 Peter 2:5.

29. Romans 14:23.

30. James 4:6–7; 1 Peter 5:5–9.

31. *Strong's Greek Lexicon*, s.v. *"G1977 epiriptō*," Blue Letter Bible, www.blueletterbible.org/lang/lexicon/lexicon.cfm?Strongs=G1977&t=ESV.

32. Psalm 38:9.

33. Matthew 11:30.

Part 2: The Community of the Beloved

1. HELPS Word-studies, s.v. "27 *agapētos*, Bible Hub, 2011, https://biblehub.com/greek/27.htm.

2. 1 John 4:11–12.

Chapter 6: There's No Brass Ring

1. John Fischer, "All Day Song (Love Him in the Morning)," *Still Life*, Light Records, 1974.

2. Christy Nockels, "A Mighty Fortress," *Life Light Up*, sixstepsrecords/Sparrow, 2009.

3. Beyoncé, "Single Ladies (Put a Ring on It)," *I Am . . . Sasha Fierce*, Columbia, 2008.

4. Christy Nockels, "Close Your Eyes," *Be Held: Lullabies for the Beloved*, Keeper's Branch Records, 2017.

5. Wikipedia, s.v. "Brass ring," https://en.wikipedia.org/wiki/Brass_ring.

6. Nockels, "Close Your Eyes."

Chapter 7: Complete My Joy

1. Romans 8:28.

2. Malachi 3:17.

3. Michael Rosen, *We're Going on a Bear Hunt* (New York: Margaret K. McElderry Books, 1989).

4. John 5:19, NIV.

5. John 14:12.

6. John 14:26.

7. Philippians 2:1–4.

8. HELPS Word-studies, s.v. "4137 *plēróō*," Bible Hub, 2011, https://biblehub.com/greek/4137.htm.

9. Dictionary.com, s.v. "relevant," www.dictionary.com/browse/relevantly.

10. Proverbs 11:25, NIV.

Chapter 8: Amaryllis Prayers

1. Christy Nockels, "My Master," *Life Light Up,* sixstepsrecords /Sparrow, 2009.

2. Zechariah 4:6.

3. *Strong's Hebrew Lexicon,* s.v. "H5643 *cether*," Blue Letter Bible, www.blueletterbible.org/lang/lexicon/lexicon.cfm?Strongs=H5643 &t=ESV.

4. C. S. Lewis, *The Lion, the Witch and the Wardrobe* Movie Tie-In Edition (Grand Rapids: Zondervan, 2005), 158.

5. Jeremiah 17:7–8.

6. John 15:2.

7. Lamentations 3:17–18.

8. Lamentations 3:24.

9. Lamentations 3:55–58.

10. You can download this letter for free at http://withyouministries .com.

11. Christy Nockels, "Amaryllis," by Christy Nockels and Kristin Hill, *The Thrill of Hope,* Keeper's Branch Records, 2016.

Part 3: The Capacity of the Beloved

1. 1 John 4:19.

2. Philippians 3:14.

3. HELPS Word-studies, s.v. "1377 *diṓkō*," Bible Hub, 2011, https://biblehub.com/greek/1377.htm.

4. *Strong's Concordance,* s.v. *"skopos,"* Bible Hub, https://biblehub.com /greek/4649.htm; "3:14 Goal," *ESV Study Bible* (Wheaton, IL: Crossway, 2008), 2286.

5. Philippians 3:12.

Chapter 9: Heart like a Honeycomb

1. Proverbs 16:9, niv.

2. Psalm 46:10.

3. Romans 5:3–5.

4. Definitions.net, s.v. "contentment," STANDS4, www.definitions .net/definition/Contentment.

5. HELPS Word-studies, s.v. "4138 *plḗrōma,*" Bible Hub, 2011, https://biblehub.com/greek/4138.htm.

6. HELPS Word-studies, s.v. "5485 *xáris,*" Bible Hub, 2011, https:// biblehub.com/greek/5485.htm.

7. Psalm 139:16, niv.

8. John 16:33.

9. William Blake, *The Complete Poetry and Prose of William Blake,* rev. ed., ed. David V. Erdman (Berkeley, CA: University of California Press, 2008), 187, 218.

10. Christy Nockels, "All That Is to Come," by Christy and Nathan Nockels, *Be Held: Lullabies for the Beloved,* Keeper's Branch Records, 2017.

11. HELPS Word-studies, s.v. "2293 *tharséō,*" Bible Hub, 2011, https://biblehub.com/greek/2293.htm.

12. Nockels, "All That Is to Come."

13. Galileo Galilei, *Dialogues Concerning Two New Sciences,* trans. Henry Crew and Alfonso de Salvio (New York: Macmillan, 1914), Online Library of Liberty, https://oll.libertyfund.org/titles/753 #Galileo_0416_515.

14. Tiju Thomas and Gaurav Tiwari, "Crushing Behaviour of Honeycomb Structure: A Review," *International Journal of Crashworthiness* (June 2018), www.researchgate.net/publication/326414870 _Crushing_Behaviour_of_Honeycomb_structure_A_Review.

15. Joanna Klein, "Electric Honeycombs Form When Nature Gets Out of Balance," *New York Times,* October 4, 2017, www.nytimes. com/2017/10/04/science/electric-honeycomb.html.

Chapter 10: Everything Is Mine in You

1. This concept was adapted from Erik Wahl, *The Spark and the Grind: Ignite the Power of Disciplined Creativity* (New York: Portfolio, 2017).
2. *Strong's Concordance,* s.v. *"nathan,"* Bible Hub, https://biblehub.com/hebrew/5414.htm.
3. Isaiah 30:21.
4. Hebrews 3:14, NLT.
5. Hebrews 2:1, NLT.
6. Romans 4:18, NIV.
7. 1 Corinthians 3:18–20.
8. 1 Corinthians 3:20, MSG.
9. 1 Corinthians 3:21–23.
10. John Piper, "All Things Are Yours" (commencement address, Bethlehem College and Seminary, Minneapolis, MN, May 17, 2013), Desiring God, www.desiringgod.org/messages/all-things -are-yours.

Chapter 11: The Power of Small

1. Mark 4:39.
2. Matthew 20:16.
3. Matthew 10:42.
4. *Strong's Concordance,* s.v. *"teleios,"* Bible Hub, https://biblehub.com /greek/5046.htm.
5. HELPS Word-studies, s.v. "5046 *téleios,"* Bible Hub, 2011, https:// biblehub.com/greek/5046.htm.
6. Matthew 5:48; *Strong's Concordance,* s.v. *"teleios."*
7. "The Heart of Worship," by Matt Redman, ThankYou Music, 1997.
8. Mark 7:36. See also Matthew 8:4; Luke 5:14; 8:56.
9. Matthew 22:37–40.

Chapter 12: Always Remember to Never Forget

1. Christy Nockels, "Always Remember to Never Forget," by Christy and Nathan Nockels, *Be Held: Lullabies for the Beloved,* Keeper's Branch Records, 2017.
2. Romans 12:2.

3. 2 Corinthians 12:9.

4. HELPS Word-studies, s.v. "5046 *téleios,*" Bible Hub, 2011, https://biblehub.com/greek/5046.htm.

5. *Strong's Concordance,* s.v. "astheneia," Bible Hub, https://biblehub.com/str/greek/769.htm.

6. Genesis 1:27.

7. Romans 12:5.

8. Hebrews 3:13–14.

9. Anabel Gillham, *The Confident Woman: Knowing Who You Are in Christ* (Eugene, OR: Harvest House, 1993), 95.

10. Galatians 2:20.

11. 2 Corinthians 1:21–22.

12. John 14:16–17.

13. Colossians 1:11.

14. HELPS Word-studies, s.v. "5281 *hypomonē,*" Bible Hub, 2011, www.biblehub.com/greek/5281.htm.

15. Ephesians 3:17–19, BSB.

16. Psalm 136.

17. Matthew 28:18–20.

18. John 1:38–39.

ABOUT THE AUTHOR

Christy Nockels is a worship leader, singer, and songwriter who has a heart to lead others to connect and communicate with God. Christy and her husband, Nathan, toured nationwide as the Christian music duo Watermark, recording five acclaimed albums.

Christy and Nathan were invited by Louie and Shelley Giglio to be a part of the first Passion Conference in Austin, Texas, which led to the couple's songwriting and leading worship for the collegiate movement for the next twenty years. Christy's voice can be heard on songs like "Waiting Here for You," and her songwriting is featured in church anthems such as "Lord, I Need You" and "Healing Is in Your Hands."

Christy now records for the couple's independent label, Keeper's Branch Records, through which they've released fan favorites like *Be Held: Lullabies for the Beloved*. Her popular podcast, *The Glorious in the Mundane,* is intentionally focused to help women in any season of life find the wonder and awe of God in the moments of the here and now.

Christy lives in Franklin, Tennessee, with her husband, Nathan, their three Beloved children, and two dogs who *think* they are Beloved children!

ABOUT THE TYPE

This book was set in Bembo, a typeface based on an old-style Roman face that was used for Cardinal Pietro Bembo's tract *De Aetna* in 1495. Bembo was cut by Francesco Griffo (1450–1518) in the early sixteenth century for Italian Renaissance printer and publisher Aldus Manutius (1449–1515). The Lanston Monotype Company of Philadelphia brought the well-proportioned letterforms of Bembo to the United States in the 1930s.

A HEARTFELT PODCAST

THE *glorious* IN THE MUNDANE

BY CHRISTY NOCKELS

— Available everywhere you listen to podcasts —

One more thing...

I don't know about you but I've realized now more than ever that we need each other in these uncertain times! The best part about the internet and even social media is that it connects the Community of the Beloved (that's us!) and makes this world feel small in the most powerful way. I've created some reader exclusive content that you can access below. I hope you'll stay in touch!

Unlock reader exclusive:

Visit www.thelifeyoulongforbook.com and enter the code: BELOVED

Connect with me on social:

Instagram: @christynockels

Facebook: @christynockelsmusic

Twitter: @christynockels

Website: christynockels.com

#thelifeyoulongforbook